# WHAT TEACHERS IN TRAINING ARE TAUGHT ABOUT READING

## The Working Papers

**Greg Brooks**
**Tom Gorman**
**Lesley Kendall**
**Alison Tate**

Research Papers submitted to the
Reading Review Working Group of
the Council for the Accreditation of Teacher Education by
the Assessment of Performance Unit Language and Communication
Team at the National Foundation for Educational Research

Published by the
National Foundation for Educational Research,
The Mere, Upton Park, Slough, Berkshire SL1 2DQ
Registered Charity No. 313392

ISBN 0 7005 1319 1

# CONTENTS

**List of Figures**

**List of Tables**

# ACKNOWLEDGEMENTS

We are grateful to all of the following individuals and groups:

- to the members of the CATE Working Group for this inquiry, in particular to the Chairperson, Professor Sir William Taylor, for advice, encouragement and support throughout the project

- to Bridie Raban, Professor of Primary Education at the University of Warwick, and to Diana Bentley and Dee Reid of the Reading and Language Information Centre, University of Reading, for advice on the institutional questionnaire

- to Mr Derek Foxman, Dr Wendy Keys and Dr Robert Stradling of NFER for comments on the text

- to Effie de Souza, who has worked with such unstinting zeal and efficiency to word-process this report

- to Mary Hargreaves for preparing the document for publication and to Tim Wright for designing the cover

- to those lecturers and students who agreed to be interviewed

- to the newly qualified teachers who completed questionnaires, especially those (the majority) who did so during their first weeks in full-time teaching

- above all, to those lecturers who, at a very inconvenient time of year, provided such detailed and informative responses to the institutional questionnaire.

## Note on authorship

Each of the individual papers is attributed to its principal author, variously Greg Brooks, Alison Tate and Tom Gorman. Lesley Kendall, the project statistician, was not the main author of any of the separate papers, but contributed significantly to most of them, and is therefore credited as an author of the whole volume.

# INTRODUCTION

In April 1991, the Secretary of State for Education and Science, Kenneth Clarke, asked the Council for the Accreditation of Teacher Education to undertake an inquiry into the preparation of student teachers to teach reading. The Department of Education and Science on behalf of the Council commissioned the National Foundation for Educational Research to obtain information on how the 92 universities, polytechnics and colleges in England, Wales and Northern Ireland which offer initial teacher training (ITT) courses prepare students to teach reading in primary and secondary schools.

The NFER inquiry began in May 1991. The research team, from the Centre for Research in Language and Communication (see Appendix A), were asked to present their final report in November 1991. The time constraints determined to some degree the research methodology that could be applied in the study.

## The research design:

It was decided to obtain the information requested by the following means:

- a review of relevant research

- a questionnaire survey of all 92 institutions of initial teacher training (ITT) in England, Wales and Northern Ireland

- a review of booklists and other relevant documentation supplied by institutions about the courses given

- a questionnaire survey of graduates newly qualified in 1991 from one course at each of 20 ITT institutions

- interviews with staff at 20 ITT institutions and with students at six.

## The information base:

The enquiries yielded the following sets of information:

- questionnaire responses covering 181 ITT courses in which the teaching of reading is one of the **core** or **compulsory** elements: these represented 74 of the 92 institutions surveyed

- (a source of information subsidiary to the institutional questionnaire was an analysis of half (85) of the booklists accompanying 170 of the responses)

- questionnaire responses from 413 newly qualified teachers

- interviews with 52 lecturers: all were language and reading specialists

- interviews with 27 students: all were Bachelor of Education (BEd) students at the beginning of the fourth year of their course.

In the course of the project, the NFER researchers involved produced five working papers setting out in detail the findings of the research. Four of these (all but the first) then provided the basis for a summary report, which in turn formed part B of the final report submitted by CATE to the DES. That final report has since been published under the title *Training Teachers to Teach Reading: a Review,* DES, 1992.

The chairperson and members of the Working Group (see Appendix B) considered that the Working Papers presented to them, prior to the preparation of the summary report, would be of interest in their own right to members of institutions offering courses in initial teacher training and all others concerned with teacher education. They therefore recommended to the DES and the NFER that these should be made more widely available.

This volume therefore contains the five working papers. They have been lightly edited, to avoid infelicities, inaccuracies and overlap, and provided with a general introduction: but otherwise they are substantially as presented to CATE. Because they were written by different authors, this volume contains no overview or integrated analysis of the findings: for that we refer readers to the NFER section of the CATE final report.

# Review of the Literature on the Preparation of Teachers to Teach Reading

by Greg Brooks

4

# REVIEW OF THE LITERATURE ON THE PREPARATION OF TEACHERS TO TEACH READING

## 1.1 Introduction

If we had adequate information on the preparation of teachers to teach reading, what would it tell us? The answers to at least the following questions:

- How much preparation do students receive?

- What are the aims of the preparation?

- What is the content of the preparation?

- How effective is the preparation?

This review of the literature on these questions is based on the following materials:

- Morrison and Austin (1977)

- the Bullock Report (DES, 1975, Chapter 23) and two HM I documents (DES, 1987; 1991)

- Wragg (1982)

- all but one (1968/69) of the *Annual Summaries of Investigations Relating to Reading* published by the International Reading Association and covering the years 1.7.64-30.6.65 up to 1.7.88-30.6.89, the latter being the latest available. Each of these volumes contains a section on 'Teacher preparation and practice'. The 24 volumes scanned contain in the sections so titled 686 summaries of journal articles. On inspection, 95 fell within the topic of this review, and all of these have been used to help form the categories employed below. However, many of the articles were relevant only to the USA, were out-of-date, or were very limited in scope (in content and/or number of people studied): only the most pertinent items will be cited and referenced here.

## 1.2 How much preparation for teaching reading do students receive?

'We consider that the basic course [on language in education for the BEd] should occupy at least 100 hours, and preferably 150' (Bullock Report (DES, 1975), p. 338).

The CATE criteria require a minimum of 100 hours for language and reading on primary BEd courses: the HMI report *Quality in Schools* (DES, 1987, p.66) stated that the average allocation for such courses was 100 hours. (Here and for later references in this paper to DES, 1987 it should be noted that that report was a summary of HMI inspections of courses before they had been scrutinised by CATE.)

For other countries, the latest information available seems to be the following.

- In Australia in 1978, only four out of 75 language courses in ITT institutions were longer than 100 hours (Morris and Cope, 1978).

- In the USA, Morrison and Austin (1977, p.7) found that 94% of colleges made a 'three-semester-hour' course in reading a compulsory requirement for all intending teachers. Flippo and Hayes (1984) found that about half of the 50 states had laws requiring two such courses for intending primary teachers, and one for secondary teachers.


## 1.3 What are the aims of the preparation?

No research has been located bearing directly on this question. Instead, what it is intended that teachers of reading should know or be able to do as a result of their preparation has to be inferred from statements about what their courses should contain, and/or from complaints about what they do not contain. For instance, Calfee (1984) argued that the foundations of literacy in English require analysis of human cognition, formal use of language (rhetoric), and the peculiarities of the English language, and stated that the materials then available for training and supporting teachers of reading in the USA gave little or no attention to these topics.

Two 'Model programmes' in reading are given in Morrison and Austin (1977, pp. 58-78) for the US context. The first is competency-based: this approach was in favour at the time, but seems later to have declined in popularity because of severe criticisms from Heath and Nielson (1974).

The Bullock Report (pp. 343-6) gives 'Two Examples of a Basic Language Course', which were not intended 'to be prescriptive but to offer starting points for discussion for teacher trainers' (p. 338).

## 1.4 What is the content of the preparation?

If full information were available, it ought to be possible to subdivide this question at least in terms of

**knowledge and skills**

**resources used**

**theoretical learning and practical experience.**

But the information available is skimpy, to put it mildly. The HMI report (DES, 1987, pp. 56-60) contains some very useful diagrams summarising the structure of several ITT courses, and illustrating the general balance within them of subject studies, curriculum studies, educational and professional studies and school experience - but all this applies to the courses as a whole and is not even intended to be revealing about the language and reading element.

In the USA, Smith, Fairbanks and Saltz (1984) surveyed 304 institutions nation-wide to gain information about their reading foundation courses. Of the 124 institutions which responded, 99 said that they had undergraduate and/or graduate level foundation courses. Respondents were asked to indicate whether specific components were included in their courses, and to rank the importance of each component. Two major sections of the survey were designed to determine emphasis on the theoretical focus (history, psychology, physiology, sociology, pedagogy, research and the reading process), as well as emphasis on a skills-related focus (skills development, communication, diagnosis and remediation, success-related factors, and current issues). Emphasis on the Reading Process appeared as the highest-ranked 'included' theoretical component (98 per cent of institutions). It also ranked highest in 'importance' (86 per cent). Historical components were ranked lowest in both inclusion and importance among the theoretical components. Among skills-related aspects, Word Recognition and Comprehension Skills were most often included (90 per cent). Diagnosis and Remediation received the lowest ranking for importance.

On a much more specific topic, Gonzales (1980) presented the results of a survey of 38 major universities in the USA designed to determine the extent to which the reading education components of their teacher certification programmes were attempting to meet the needs of linguistic minority children. He concluded that the institutions were by and large addressing these needs.

## 1.5 How effective is students' preparation?

This, perhaps the key question, is difficult to tackle directly, though the fifth subcategory below shows that at least one such attempt has been made. The first four subcategories highlight a small selection of the attempts at indirect measures.

a)    How far are students influenced by memories of how they themselves learnt to read? (This can be seen as implying 'How far has their training countered or broadened that influence?')

Wendelin, Zinck and Carter (1981) replicated and updated a 1949 study designed to elicit titles of books that were the personal favourites of teachers, as well as to determine teachers' opinions regarding 'best' and 'most popular' books. The sample was 733 teachers in five states. The result suggested that what was read and enjoyed in childhood appeared to influence teachers' judgements of what should be read now.

Artley (1975) asked 100 students at the University of Missouri to recall effective and ineffective teaching of reading in their own childhood experience. The most frequent favourable memory was of being read to by teachers. Amongst bad memories were too much skill drill, repetitious workbook pages and round-robin reading. It may be that some movements in the teaching of reading are influenced at a deep level by such memories.

b)    How well prepared do students consider themselves?

There are two relevant pieces of British research, though neither is particularly recent. Goodacre and Clark (1971) analysed the results of a questionnaire sent to primary teachers in an English industrial city, an English county, and a Scottish county containing both rural and urban areas. When asked to assess their teacher training in reading, 47 per cent of Scottish teachers and 21 per cent of English teachers claimed that they were dissatisfied with it, and only 15 per cent and 10 per cent respectively expressed satisfaction.

Bassey (1981) reported answers from 131 Nottinghamshire primary teachers who had obtained a Teacher's Certificate or BEd between 1942 and 1978 to the question 'In your opinion, how effective was your course in preparing you for teaching children to read?' Responses were: Good, 29 per cent; Middling, 18 per cent; Inadequate, 50 per cent (Not able to answer, three per cent).

Much more work has been done in the USA. A highly unusual approach was taken by Deiulio (1973). He studied the graffiti found on the desks in college classrooms in a building used for professional education courses for the previous 25 years. Students' feelings were judged as tending to be negative, and the author suggested several changes in curricular structure as a result.

8

From a survey of 404 people who had been undergraduates in education in 37 US colleges or universities in 22 states, Cheek (1982) found (among other things) that the most helpful topic in undergraduate reading courses had been 'How to plan a reading lesson'. However, another article apparently emanating from the same research (Collins-Cheek, 1983) reports that classroom teaching experience was the most significant factor in job preparation, and that diagnosis and prescriptive teaching or remediation were the two most helpful reading courses taken.

Wendelin and Murphy (1986) reported that, at the end of teaching practice, of 125 students surveyed 79 per cent felt that their preparation to teach reading had been adequate. And Alvermann and Smith (1984) reported that 119 intending primary teachers most frequently cited familiarity with basic, general classroom diagnosis and the use of simulated activities as the major components of their reading education courses which had been of value.

c)    How well prepared are students considered by others?

Here the evidence is qualitative rather than quantitative, and British rather than American, and takes the form of statements in official reports. The Bullock Report devoted a substantial paragraph (23.3, pp.331-2) to a list of reported shortcomings in current initial courses. Among them were:

- an uncertain relationship between theory and practice

- students rarely having the opportunity to study an individual child's reading

- great variation in the extent to which students received help from the cooperating teacher and from the supervisor

- insufficient attention to reading beyond the initial stages.

Twelve years on, the earlier of the two HMI reports cited in the Introduction (DES, 1987) gives the impression that the reading element of primary BEd courses was generally satisfactory (p.66). The sections on primary PGCE courses (p.68) and on the training of secondary teachers (p.119) make no overt reference to reading - but this is perhaps not surprising in a brief report covering so much ground.

The generally favourable picture of the reading element in primary BEd/ BA(Ed) courses is implied again in the second HMI report (DES, 1991, p.7).

d)    How much do students know when they have completed their courses?

By far the most comprehensive database on this question would be students' continuous and final assessments, but no information is available on this; and in any case the information would be both impressionistic in the case of most forms of assessment, and too general to isolate knowledge about reading.

There have, however, been several attempts in the USA to devise instruments that are both standardised and specific to reading, or indeed to particular aspects of it, especially phonics. Narang (1978) reviewed previous work of this sort and concluded that almost all of it was deeply flawed. For primary teachers, there was only one test which was comprehensive in scope and statistically acceptable, the *Inventory of Teacher Knowledge of Reading* (Artley and Hardin, 1975). This consisted of 95 multiple-choice items intended to cover the following areas:

the reading act

preparation for reading

word identification

comprehension and critical reading

reading in the content areas

reading interests and tastes

corrective procedures.

For secondary level, Narang (1980) himself developed a 45-item multiple-choice *Test of Teacher Knowledge of Reading* covering the nature of reading, reading materials, reading skills, instructional strategies, and measurement and evaluation. Neither test seems to have been much researched since, and both seem unlikely to have stood the test of time.

One piece of British work in this area has to be mentioned. Morris (1985) gave a quiz testing knowledge of the phonological and spelling systems of English to 275 students at an ITT institution. The reported results were poor, and were used to argue for greater emphasis on linguistics in ITT course. However, it is known that the instrument used was severely criticised by linguists, who therefore thought little of the results, while not dissenting from the conclusion about linguistics.

e)   How high are the correlations between students' preparation and their effectiveness as teachers of reading?

Research in this area is obviously both very difficult to mount, and fraught with conceptual and statistical problems. What, to begin with, constitutes effective teaching of reading? One piece of relevant research which has been identified can illustrate the difficulties. Lovelace, Collins and de Santi (1984) examined the relationship between student teachers' performance on the (US) National Teacher Examinations (NTE) and their actual classroom performance. Twenty students were selected from a population of 76 (at one institution?). Each subject was observed three times for two hours, and classroom performance was evaluated in relation to teaching plans and materials, classroom procedures, and interpersonal skills. One trained observer viewed all subjects using the Teacher Performance Assessment Instruments (TPAI), which were developed in previous research. Cumulative grade point average (GPA) and scores from the ACT (American College Test?) were also used in the analysis. There were significant correlations between GPA and performance on three subtests of the NTE. However, classroom performance was not highly correlated with performance on the NTE.

## 1.6  Conclusions

This review is cursory, but it suggests that the research base in this area is very limited, and that much of the necessary work remains to be done.

# References

ALVERMANN, D.E. and SMITH, L.C. (1984). 'How reading field experience students view the observation/evaluation process.' In: McNINCH, G.H. (Ed) *Reading Teacher Education*. Fourth Yearbook of the American Reading Forum, pp.26-7.

ARTLEY, A.S. (1975). 'Good teachers of reading - who are they?', *The Reading Teacher*, **29**, 26-31.

ARTLEY, A.S. and HARDIN, V. (1975). *Inventory of Teacher Knowledge of Reading* (revised edn). Columbus, Mo: Lucas Brothers Publishers.

BASSEY, M. (1981). '131 primary school teachers' opinions about their college training', *Educational Research*, **23**, 3, 225-7.

CALFEE, R. (1984). 'Applying cognitive psychology to educational practice: the mind of the reading teacher.' In: BOWLER, R.F. (Ed) *Annuals of Dyslexia*, Vol. 34. Baltimore, MD: The Orton Dyslexia Society, 219-240.

CHEEK, M.C. (1982). 'Preservice education in reading: what do the teachers say?', *Reading Psychology*, **3**, 25-35.

COLLINS-CHEEK, M.D. (1983) 'Graduate programs in reading: What do graduates say about them?' *Reading Improvement*, **20**, 200-80.

DEIULIO, A.M. (1973). 'Desk top graffiti: scratching beneath the surface', *Journal of Research and Development in Education*, **7**, 100-4.

DES (1975). *A Language for Life* (The Bullock Report). London: HMSO.

DES (1987). *Quality in Schools: the Initial Training of Teachers*. London: HMSO.

DES (1991). *The Professional Training of Primary School Teachers.A Report by HMI*. London: DES.

FLIPPO, R.F. and HAYES, D.A. (1984). 'Preparation in reading and educator certification: requirements, needs, issues.' In: McNINCH, G.H. (Ed) *Reading Teacher Education*. Fourth Yearbook of the American Reading Forum, pp.27-9.

GONZALES, P.C. (1980). 'Teacher preparation: meeting the needs of the limited English speaking student', *Reading World*, **19**, 375-82.

GOODACRE, E.J. and CLARK, M.M. (1971). 'Initial approaches to teaching reading in Scottish and English schools', *Reading*, **5**, 2, 15-21.

HEATH, R.W. and NIELSON, M.A. (1974). 'The research basis for performance-based teacher education', *Review of Educational Research*, **44**, 4, 463-84.

LOVELACE, T., COLLINS, M. and de SANTI, R. (1984). 'Predicting and evaluating student teachers' performance in reading instruction.' In: McNINCH, G.H. (Ed) *Reading Teacher Education*. Fourth Yearbook of the American Reading Forum, pp.59-61.

MORRIS, A. and COPE, R.G. (1978). 'Preparation of Australian primary teachers in the teaching of reading', *South Pacific Journal of Teacher Education*, **6**, 1, 69-73.

MORRIS, J.M. (1985). 'Before a byte, the LITE approach to literacy.' In: Ewing, J. (Ed) *Reading and the New Technologies*. London: Heinemann Educational Books, pp.49-55.

MORRISON, M. and AUSTIN, M.C. (1977). *The Torch Lighters Revisited*. Newark, DE: International Reading Association.

NARANG, H.L. (1978). 'Measurement of knowledge of reading', Reading Horizons, **18**, 116-23.

NARANG, H.L. (1980). 'Factors associated with teacher knowledge of reading at the secondary level', *Reading Horizons*, **21**, 5-60.

SMITH, P.K., FAIRBANKS, M.M. and SALTZ, M. (1984). 'Status and content of reading foundation courses', *Reading Improvement*, **21**, 232-9.

WENDELIN, K.H. and MURPHY, C.C. (1986). 'Preservice teachers' perceptions of their reading methods preparation', *Reading Improvement*, **23**, 21-6.

WENDELIN, K.H., ZINCK, R.A. and CARTER, S.M. (1981). 'Teachers' memories and opinions of children's books: a research update', *Language Arts*, **58**, 416-24.

WRAGG, E.C. (1982). *A Review of Research in Teacher Education*. Windsor: NFER-NELSON.

# The Institutional Questionnaire

**by Greg Brooks**

# THE INSTITUTIONAL QUESTIONNAIRE

## 2.1 The research design

### 2.1.1 The approach

This questionnaire was devised in May 1991 and sent out in June to all 92 of the higher education institutions in England, Wales and Northern Ireland which had initial teacher training (ITT) courses running in the academic year 1990/91. The questionnaire is reproduced in this volume as Appendix C. Sufficient copies were sent to cover all of the approximately 350 ITT courses offered by those institutions.

The main part of the questionnaire asked for 'information only on the training in the teaching of reading that ALL students on the course are exposed to, i.e. the MINIMUM or CORE or COMPULSORY coverage of reading in the course'. However, the questionnaire also asked for copies of course documents, including booklists issued to students, and details of optional reading courses and/or reading elements in subject specialisms.

### 2.1.2 The sample

**Questionnaires**

Of the 92 institutions which had ITT courses running in the academic year 1990/ 91, 88 (96 per cent) responded.

The number of questionnaires returned was 225. Of these, 21 were blanks or duplicates. A further 23 proved to relate only to specialist, optional or non-core elements in the courses they described: these were left unanalysed. Therefore, 181 questionnaires from 74 institutions were coded for full analysis.

These coded responses represented just over 50 per cent of the approximately 350 ITT courses current at the time. It is known that in a number of cases non-response was due to the course having no compulsory or core reading elements; the 181 responses therefore represented a higher, but not precisely known, percentage of eligible ITT courses.

**Course documents**

The amounts of material submitted with the questionnaire varied from a couple of sheets to a stack several times the size of this report. The bulk of this material could not be analysed within the timescale of this project, but a number of illustrative details have been drawn from this material and will be found in various parts of this volume.

The one section of the material that could be handled was the reading lists or booklists supplied. The report of the booklist analysis is included in this volume as Working Paper 3.

## 2.1.3 The structure of the questionnaire sample

Of the 181 courses covered by the fully coded responses, 172 (95 per cent) were full-time. In what follows, therefore, no further analyses are carried out in terms of the full-time/part-time distinction. For some purposes below, comparisons are made between four-year BEd and one-year PGCE courses: no part-time courses occurred in these categories.

Question 5 of the questionnaire asked for the qualification aimed at by the course. For the purposes of analysis, all first degree courses (BEd, BA + CertEd, BSc + CertEd, etc.) were amalgamated into one category; similarly all PGCE and other postgraduate courses (including Articled Teacher schemes) were amalgamated into another. The resulting breakdown was as follows:

| | | |
|---|---|---|
| First degree courses (BEd, etc.) | 80 | (44 per cent) |
| Postgraduate courses (PGCE, etc.) | 101 | (56 per cent) |

In all further analyses, these two categories will be referred to for convenience simply as 'BEd' and 'PGCE', respectively.

The breakdown of the courses by length in years (question 3) is shown in Figure 2.1.1.

*Figure 2.1.1    Institutional questionnaire responses by type and length of course*

Type of course

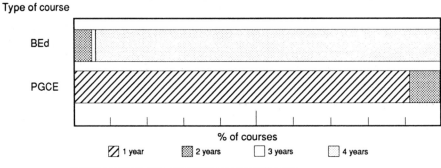

Results based on responses from 80 BEd and 101 PGCE courses

Some data from the questionnaire (e.g. from question 8 on time allocations in different years) must clearly be analysed according to length of course in years. However, it would be pointless to report separately on the small numbers of two-year and three-year courses. Some analyses will therefore be reported only for four-year BEd and one-year PGCE courses, which represent 94 per cent of the 80 BEds and 92 per cent of the 101 PGCEs.

Question 6 asked for the age-range of pupils that students were being prepared to teach. The courses covered 20 different target age-ranges, which were grouped into four categories, as shown in Table 2.1.1.

**Table 2.1.1    Age-range categories**

| Category | Lower limit(s) | Upper limit(s) | N |
|---|---|---|---|
| Early years | 3,4,5 | 7,8,9 | 39 |
| Early years + Junior | 3,4,5 | 11,12 | 83 |
| Junior | 7 | 11,12 | 34 |
| Secondary | 11,12 | 14,16,18,19,'adult' | 25 |
| | | Total | 181 |

Some observations should be made at this point about the small number of secondary responses. Many more than 25 secondary courses were current in 1990-91. It may well be that the major reason for non-response in this category was that in many secondary courses no training in the teaching of reading was provided for **all** students on the course. In a few cases this is known to be so; a number of the secondary responses received but excluded from the analysis stated that training in the teaching of reading was given only to specialists in various subjects.

The 25 secondary responses represented 14 per cent overall of those analysed. The number of secondary responses to particular items on the questionnaire, however, fell at times to seven or fewer. Though many of the analyses reported in the rest of this paper are not differentiated by age-range, in most cases this makes little difference to the interpretation. Where this might be the case, a caveat is entered.

The breakdown of the four age-range categories by type and length of course is shown in Figure 2.1.2 overleaf.

Age range of course

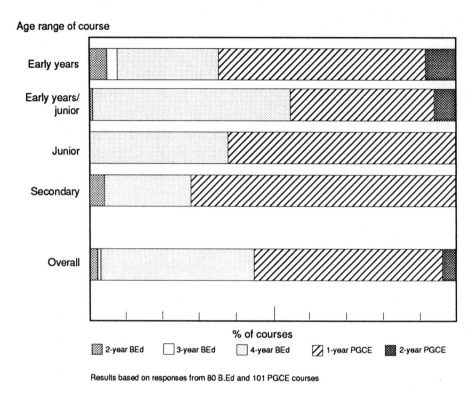

% of courses

▨ 2-year BEd    ☐ 3-year BEd    ▨ 4-year BEd    ▨ 1-year PGCE    ▨ 2-year PGCE

Results based on responses from 80 B.Ed and 101 PGCE courses

In the rest of this paper on the institutional questionnaire, many analyses will be presented in terms of type and length of course, rather than in terms of age-range.

## 2.2 Staff involved in teaching about the teaching of reading

### 2.2.1 Numbers

Question 7a asked how many staff were involved in preparing students to teach reading on the core/compulsory elements of the course. Figure 2.2.1 gives these figures by type of course.

**Figure 2.2.1**    *Percentages of BEd and PGCE courses having numbers of staff from 1-7 or more*

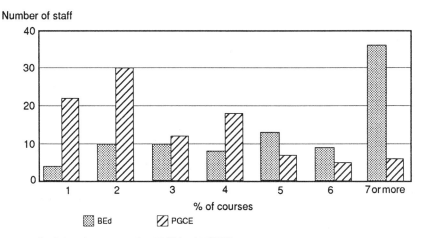

Results based on responses from 77 BEd and 96 PGCE courses

There was a tendency for BEd courses to have more staff teaching about reading: but, given the much greater average length of BEd courses, the differential was perhaps not as great as might be expected.

### 2.2.2 Experience and qualifications

The second part of question 7 asked how many of the staff teaching on the course had

- recent experience of teaching reading in early years
- other recent experience of teaching reading in schools
- experience of teaching pupils with learning difficulties
- postgraduate qualifications in linguistics or applied linguistics, psychology, and other relevant subjects.

The last part of question 7b invited respondents to write in any other relevant postgraduate qualification held by staff involved in preparing students to teach reading. The most frequently mentioned qualifications among the 127 responses to this question are shown in Table 2.2.1.

*Table 2.2.1    Other relevant postgraduate qualifications of staff*

| Qualification | Number of courses |
| --- | --- |
| Language in Education | 25 |
| Master's degree in Language | 25 |
| Other master's degrees | 31 |
| PhD | 11 |
| Advanced Certificate or Diploma | 9 |

Based on responses from 127 courses

The first two categories could perhaps have been entered higher in question 7b under 'Linguistics/applied linguistics' - but it may be that respondents were using a strict definition of 'applied linguistics'.

Some respondents gave no answers to any part of question 7b: in these cases, the data for all parts of question 7b were treated as missing.

Even then, data on the **absolute** numbers of staff on courses possessing (or not possessing) the various forms of experience and qualification would not be meaningful: they need to be related to the total number of staff on the course involved in preparing students to teach reading. For each part of question 7b, therefore, we calculated the proportion (percentage) of staff on each course with the experience or qualification. These data are summarised in Figures 2.2.2 and 2.2.3 for BEd and PGCE courses respectively.

*Figure 2.2.2    4-year BEd courses:  Proportions of staff with various forms of teaching experience/postgraduate qualifications*

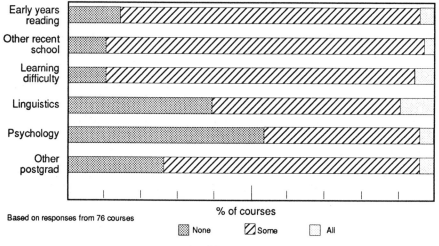

Based on responses from 76 courses

% of courses

☷ None      ▨ Some      ☐ All

22

*Figure 2.2.3*   **PGCE courses:  Proportions of staff with various forms of teaching experience/postgraduate qualifications**

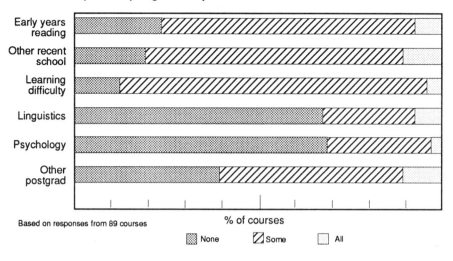

Based on responses from 89 courses

% of courses

▦ None     ▨ Some     ☐ All

These figures show that, for each of the types of experience and qualification mentioned, at least ten per cent of each type of course had no staff with that experience or qualification.  The position was most marked for postgraduate qualifications in psychology: over 50 per cent of both types of course had no staff so qualified involved in teaching about reading.  (It should be said that several of the courses with no staff with experience of teaching reading in early years were secondary.)

On the other hand, on ten per cent of PGCE courses, all the staff had other recent experience of teaching reading. In a similar percentage of PGCE courses, all the staff had postgraduate qualifications.

The picture is therefore uneven.  Given the small numbers of staff on some courses, this is inevitable: but some institutions might need to consider the balance of qualifications and experience of the staff involved in these courses.

## 2.3  Time allocated to teaching about the teaching of reading

Question 8a asked, for each year of the course, how many hours of staff-student contact time were allocated to language, including reading; and question 8b asked how many hours within those totals were allocated specifically to reading.

The absolute values given were extremely varied.  As already explained, data from these questions are examined only for the two large categories of course, namely four-year BEds and one-year PGCEs.  Tables 2.3.1 and 2.3.2 give the results for these two types of course, for language and reading respectively.

**Table 2.3.1**  *Mean hours and range of staff-student contact time devoted to LANGUAGE (four-year BEd and one-year PGCE courses only)*

| Type of course | Year of course | Mean | Range |
|---|---|---|---|
| Four-year BEd | 1 | 29 | 0 - 100 |
| | 2 | 27 | 0 - 120 |
| | 3 | 23 | 0 - 84 |
| | 4 | 11 | 0 - 120 |
| | All years combined | 90 | 13 - 265 |

Results based on 70 courses

| | | | |
|---|---|---|---|
| One-year PGCE | | 57 | 6 - 160 |

Results based on 82 courses

**Table 2.3.2**  *Mean hours and range of staff-student contact time devoted to READING (four-year BEd and one-year PGCE courses only)*

| Type of course | Year of course | Mean | Range |
|---|---|---|---|
| Four-year BEd | 1 | 11 | 0 - 60 |
| | 2 | 10 | 0 - 40 |
| | 3 | 9 | 0 - 30 |
| | 4 | 3 | 0 - 30 |
| | All years combined | 90 | 3 - 114 |

Results based on 68 courses

| | | | |
|---|---|---|---|
| One-year PGCE | | 22 | 2 - 100 |

Results based on 81 courses

## Four-year BEd courses

Most four-year BEd courses gave 60 or more hours of staff-student contact time to language overall, and, about half gave over 30 hours to reading. Indeed, 15 per cent of courses were allocating over 120 hours to language, while 10 per cent courses were allocating less than 60 hours - most, but not all, of these were secondary.

24

The range of number of hours allocated to reading was wide. Eighty per cent of four-year BEd courses allocated between 16 and 47 hours to reading: to put this another way, only ten per cent of such courses allocated less than 16 hours to reading, while ten per cent allocated more than 47 hours. The mean number of hours was 34.

Within four-year BEd courses, time for language and reading was distributed fairly evenly across years 1-3, but the average allocation in the fourth year was much lower. In the fourth year, most courses allocated no time at all to reading, and barely any to other aspects of language.

### One-year PGCE courses

Of the 82 one-year PGCE courses responding here, most gave 60 or more hours to language, and about half gave 20 hours or more to reading.

Again, the range of number of hours was wide. Eighty per cent of one-year PGCE courses allocated between 6 and 35 hours to reading: ten per cent allocated less than six hours, and ten per cent allocated more than 35 hours. The mean number of hours was 22.

## 2.4  Approaches to early reading

### 2.4.1 Information requested

The complex and significant area of approaches to early reading was addressed in question 9a, which presented respondents with a list of nine approaches to the teaching of early reading, and with spaces to write in up to three more; and then asked them, for each of the topics, to indicate how much attention it was given on the course. Three indications of amount of attention were requested:

- the year(s) of the course in which the topic was addressed
- the teaching/delivery modes used
- hours of staff-student contact time, and an estimate of student non-contact hours, involved in addressing the topic.

The opportunity to write in extra topics was taken up by 128 respondents. The additional topic that was most frequently mentioned (by 38 respondents) was (one or more aspects of) emergent literacy. This number was too small to justify treating this as a tenth topic within the analyses.

Many respondents felt that it was inappropriate to specify the numbers of hours (in terms of contact and non-contact time) devoted to the teaching of particular topics; others found it difficult to provide the evidence requested. Data on hours of contact and non-contact time are therefore not reported here. Intelligible information about the topics dealt with in each year and the teaching modes adopted for the purpose was, however, provided.

## 2.4.2 Four-year BEd courses

### A. Attention given across years

The percentages of four-year BEd courses in which attention was given to the nine named topics are shown in Table 2.4.1.

**Table 2.4.1** *Percentage of four-year BEd courses giving attention to various approaches in different years.*

| Approach | Year 1 | Year 2 | Year 3 | Year 4 |
|----------|--------|--------|--------|--------|
| Phonics | 53 | 56 | 52 | 23 |
| Look and say | 53 | 54 | 42 | 21 |
| Lang. exp | 46 | 54 | 50 | 24 |
| Real books | 54 | 61 | 48 | 27 |
| Clues | 56 | 58 | 54 | 32 |
| Integrated | 52 | 61 | 62 | 33 |
| Parents | 39 | 50 | 50 | 27 |
| Materials | 48 | 54 | 52 | 24 |
| Schemes | 35 | 52 | 44 | 21 |

Results based on 78 courses

These figures seem remarkably consistent, and to tell a general story of attention distributed mainly across years 1-3, with fewer courses giving the topics attention in the fourth year.

The data in Table 2.4.1 need to be interpreted, however, in the light of those given in Table 2.4.2. That table shows, for each of the topics, the percentage of four-year BEd courses in which attention was given to the topic, in different numbers of years.

26

**Table 2.4.2** *Percentage of four-year BEd courses giving attention to various approaches in different numbers of years*

| Approach | 0 | 1 out of 4 | 2 out of 4 | 3 out of 4 | All |
|---|---|---|---|---|---|
| Phonics | 15 | 20 | 39 | 18 | 8 |
| Look and say | 15 | 29 | 33 | 15 | 8 |
| Lang.exp | 20 | 20 | 36 | 15 | 9 |
| Real books | 17 | 14 | 42 | 17 | 11 |
| Clues | 15 | 17 | 35 | 20 | 14 |
| Integrated | 15 | 12 | 38 | 20 | 15 |
| Parents | 20 | 23 | 36 | 14 | 8 |
| Materials | 17 | 21 | 38 | 15 | 9 |
| Schemes | 20 | 30 | 35 | 9 | 6 |

Results based on 78 courses

The evidence indicates that at least 15 per cent of the courses did not give attention to the topic of 'real books', and a similar proportion did not report giving specific attention to 'phonics'. A similar pattern is apparent for the other approaches listed.

Comparatively few courses gave the various topics attention in all four years.

## B.    Delivery modes

For each of the nine named approaches to early reading, respondents were also asked to indicate which of five teaching/delivery modes were used in addressing that topic. The results for four-year BEd courses are shown in Table 2.4.3.

**Table 2.4.3** *Percentages of courses using various teaching modes, by topic (four-year BEd courses only)*

| Topic | Lectures/ seminars | Guided reading | Teaching practice | School-based projects | Essays |
|---|---|---|---|---|---|
| Phonics | 92 | 83 | 59 | 58 | 47 |
| Look-and-say | 91 | 80 | 53 | 52 | 39 |
| Language experience | 88 | 77 | 59 | 52 | 41 |
| Real books | 88 | 77 | 56 | 50 | 42 |
| Use of clues | 89 | 79 | 71 | 61 | 38 |
| Integrated approach | 86 | 74 | 70 | 58 | 50 |
| Involving parents | 82 | 77 | 42 | 30 | 26 |
| Selecting materials | 91 | 79 | 70 | 64 | 42 |
| Selecting schemes | 92 | 67 | 53 | 45 | 29 |

Results based on 66 courses

The columns for the teaching/delivery modes have been rearranged from the sequence in the questionnaire, in order to bring out even more clearly the consistent rank-ordering of the modes across approaches. In over three-quarters of the institutions, lectures and guided reading were used to teach the aspects of reading referred to. Teaching practice and practical or school-based projects provided the context in which these aspects of reading were taught in at least half of the courses (with the exception of activities involving parents).

An apparent inconsistency between Tables 2.4.2 and 2.4.3 should be explained. If 15 per cent of courses were giving no attention to phonics, it would seem impossible at first sight for 92 per cent of courses to be dealing with phonics through lectures. However, the results in Table 2.4.3 are based on fewer courses: most of those responding 'Not at all' for Table 2.4.2 did not provide data for Table 2.4.3.

### 2.4.3 One-year PGCE courses

#### A. Attention given

Those answering for these courses had of course only one year for which to indicate attention to topics. Among the 93 one-year PGCEs, for each of the nine approaches, between 55 and 60 per cent of the respondents indicated it was given attention on the course.

#### B. Delivery modes

Table 2.4.4 presents the data for teaching/delivery modes for one-year PGCE courses (as Table 2.4.3 above did for four-year BEds).

Table 2.4.4    Percentages of courses using various teaching modes, by topic (one-year PGCE courses only)

| Topic | Lectures/ seminars | Guided reading | Teaching practice | School-based projects | Essays |
|---|---|---|---|---|---|
| Phonics | 82 | 74 | 56 | 50 | 27 |
| Look-and-say | 77 | 69 | 50 | 45 | 23 |
| Language experience | 74 | 68 | 54 | 47 | 28 |
| Real books | 78 | 73 | 53 | 51 | 30 |
| Use of clues | 78 | 68 | 56 | 53 | 24 |
| Integrated approach | 78 | 68 | 60 | 51 | 33 |
| Involving parents | 72 | 68 | 40 | 28 | 19 |
| Selecting materials | 81 | 69 | 55 | 50 | 27 |
| Selecting schemes | 74 | 68 | 49 | 47 | 22 |

Results based on 78 courses

As with four-year BEds, the rank-ordering of modes is totally consistent. And again involving parents seems to have been the topic receiving least attention in the 'active' modes (school-based projects and teaching practice)

### 2.4.4  Reading schemes

A supplementary section of question 9a asked which reading schemes, if any, were recommended. There were 355 responses, relating to 161 courses; all but seven of the responses were from primary courses. A group of 20 respondents (including five from secondary courses) said simply that no schemes were recommended. None of these respondents went on to mention any reading schemes by name. A group of 49 respondents said principles for evaluating reading schemes were taught, and a further group of 48 said the schemes most widely used in schools and/or most recently published were available for students to evaluate. Six respondents made both comments).

Among those who did make recommendations, the three most frequently mentioned English-language schemes were *Story Chest* (47), *Oxford Reading Tree* (33) and *Ginn 360* (29). For Welsh, eight respondents mentioned *Cynllun y Ddraig*.

### 2.4.5  The mix of approaches

Question 9b asked what students were taught about selecting, sequencing or combining different approaches to teaching reading. The most frequently mentioned responses are shown in Figure 2.4.1.

**Figure 2.4.1**   **What students are taught about selecting, sequencing or combining approaches to teaching reading**

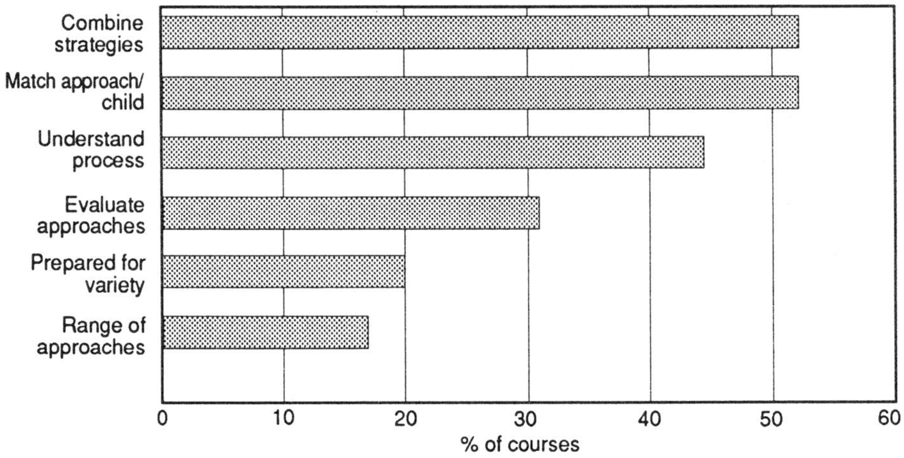

Results based upon responses from 168 courses.
Respondents could make more than one comment.

### 2.4.6 Conclusions

The general impression that would be gained from the answers to the various parts of question 9 and from the corresponding interview data is that eclecticism rules. All the approaches to early reading listed in 9a are given attention in over 80 per cent of courses. The approaches to early reading are taught through a variety of modes, though some modes are less used for some topics. Several respondents to question 9b said explicitly that 'A range of approaches is taught'. A few actually wrote in 'An eclectic approach' at the end of the grid in question 9a.

Besides displaying this open-mindedness, it seems that lecturers encourage their students to take a critically intelligent approach: this is the clear implication of the four most frequent responses to question 9b, and of the answers to the question about reading schemes in terms of teaching principles for evaluating schemes and of making them available to students for evaluation. From an interview with a group of five staff at one institution, it was clear that the language and reading syllabus was varied and rich: learning about several teaching methods arose quite naturally from this mix.

Yet this impartiality seems neither absolute nor entirely credible. It is not absolute because some respondents recommended at least one reading scheme. It is not entirely credible because of points which arose during other interviews. At several institutions it was clear that, though lecturers **mentioned** a range of approaches, they **favoured** some over others. One lecturer interviewed distinguished between 'code-centred approaches' (principally phonics) and 'meaning-centred approaches', and clearly preferred the latter. From the interview with students at the same institution, it was clear they were in no doubt about this stance. At another institution, the students interviewed said the staff distinguished between 'traditional' approaches (phonics, look-and-say, reading schemes) and 'modern' approaches (language experience, real books), and that the staff made clear their preference for the 'modern' approaches.

## 2.5. Developing Reading

Developing reading was the focus of question 10, an open-ended item. A very wide range of responses was given; the most frequently mentioned are summarised in Figure 2.5.1.

**Figure 2.5.1**   *Attention given to developing and extending reading (most frequently mentioned responses)*

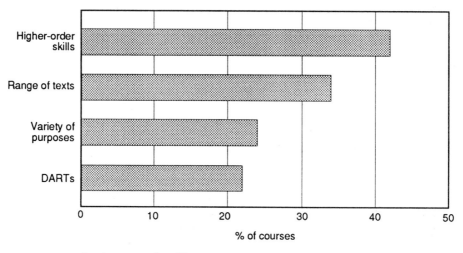

% of courses

Based on responses from 173 courses.
Respondents could make more than one comment.

The questionnaire data therefore show some respondents claiming to cover the major themes in this area, and at least one of the better-known specific techniques.

31

## 2.6 Assessment of reading

### 2.6.1 Information requested

This area was dealt with in question 11. The first section was similar in format to question 9a, but its content was a list of five assessment-related topics, with spaces for respondents to write in up to four more. However, none of the additional topics entered at the end of the grid was mentioned by enough respondents to justify analysis. Again, as with question 9a, the data given about hours of contact and non-contact time are not reported.

### 2.6.2 Four-year BEd courses

**A.    Attention given across years.**

The percentages of four-year BEd courses in which attention was given to the five topics in Years 1-4 are shown in Table 2.6.1.

*Table 2.6.1 Percentage of courses giving attention to various approaches in different years*

| Approach | Year 1 | Year 2 | Year 3 | Year 4 |
|---|---|---|---|---|
| Informal methods | 36 | 51 | 54 | 26 |
| Published tests | 17 | 44 | 46 | 20 |
| NCA: Teacher Assessment | 36 | 53 | 60 | 43 |
| NCA: Standard Assessment Tasks | 24 | 39 | 49 | 39 |
| Records of Achievement | 44 | 56 | 66 | 41 |

Results based on 70 courses

Many courses focused on assessment in Years 2 and 3. Table 2.6.2 shows the numbers of four-year BEd courses on which attention was given to each of the assessment topics, by number of years.

**Table 2.6.2**    *Percentage of courses giving attention to various approaches in different numbers of years*

| Approach | 0 | 1 out of 4 | 2 out of 4 | 3 out of 4 | All |
|---|---|---|---|---|---|
| Informal records | 14 | 29 | 39 | 13 | 6 |
| Published tests | 24 | 41 | 20 | 11 | 3 |
| NCA: Teacher Assessment | 13 | 23 | 36 | 17 | 11 |
| NCA: Standard Assessment Tasks | 24 | 27 | 29 | 14 | 6 |
| Keeping records | 10 | 21 | 36 | 17 | 16 |

Results based on 70 courses

The topic of published reading tests appeared to be given no attention in nearly a quarter of the courses. One assumes that the topic of Standard Assessment Tasks is given more attention now than at the time of the survey.

There is some evidence that on many courses consideration of assessment issues, particularly published tests and Standard Assessment Tasks, was not begun until the second or even the third year. The full tables (not reproduced here) show that there were even a small number of institutions where all consideration of assessment was concentrated into the fourth year. Such institutions may consider that students should encounter pedagogical issues before assessment.

## B.   Delivery modes

In relation to assessment, as with approaches to early reading, respondents gave information on delivery modes. The results are shown in Table 2.6.3.

**Table 2.6.3**    *Percentages of courses using various teaching modes, by assessment topic (four-year BEd courses only)*

| Topic | Lectures/ seminars | Guided reading | Teaching practice | School-based projects | Essays |
|---|---|---|---|---|---|
| Informal methods | 86 | 76 | 73 | 48 | 34 |
| Published tests | 70 | 44 | 24 | 27 | 13 |
| NCA: Teacher Assessment | 84 | 69 | 74 | 48 | 36 |
| NCA: Standard Assessment Tasks | 76 | 57 | 40 | 30 | 23 |
| Keeping records | 86 | 70 | 80 | 57 | 30 |

Results based on 70 courses

It would seem that students on relatively few courses had the opportunity to focus on the use of published reading tests, whether in the course of teaching practice or through school-based projects.

## 2.6.3 One-year PGCE courses

### A. Attention given

Among the 93 such courses, for each of the five assessment topics, between 45 and 55 per cent of respondents indicated it was given attention on the course.

### B. Delivery modes

Table 2.6.4 presents the data for teaching modes for one-year PGCE courses.

**Table 2.6.4** Percentages of courses using various teaching modes, by assessment topic (one-year PGCE courses only)

| Topic | Lectures/ seminars | Guided reading | Teaching practice | School-based projects | Essays |
|---|---|---|---|---|---|
| Informal methods | 83 | 74 | 66 | 52 | 24 |
| Published tests | 62 | 43 | 20 | 21 | 7 |
| NCA: Teacher Assessment | 75 | 60 | 58 | 52 | 22 |
| NCA: Standard Assessment Tasks | 68 | 47 | 37 | 28 | 14 |
| Keeping records | 82 | 68 | 67 | 47 | 26 |

Results based on 76 courses

On the whole the evidence shows a similar pattern to that observed in the BEd courses. As in the BEd courses, published reading tests were mentioned but not often made the subject of student activity. This was also true, though to a lesser extent, of SATs.

## 2.6.4 Exceptional children

The supplementary question 11b asked in what ways the course ensured that students were equipped to deal with gifted children and those with special needs. There were 167 responses. Many of the ideas mentioned concentrated on the methods staff used to put these topics over, or repeated key phrases from the question. The two most frequently mentioned informative answers were 'planning for individual needs' (46 per cent) and 'identifying needs' (39 per cent).

### 2.6.5 Conclusion

A few years ago an HMI report (DES, 1987) stated that assessment was a neglected area in many ITT courses. The questionnaire data presented in this section seem to suggest little change in this situation.

## 2.7 School Experience

Question 12 asked what opportunities existed for students to practise the teaching of reading during school experience. The responses are summarised in Figure 2.7.1.

**Figure 2.7.1**   *Opportunities to practice teaching reading on school experience (most frequently mentioned responses)*

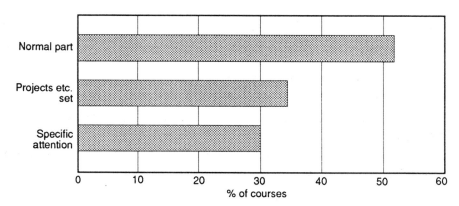

Results based on responses from 169 courses
Respondents could make more than one comment

One can deduce from the evidence that for many students opportunities to practise teaching reading are assumed but not specifically planned for. A breakdown by age-range suggested that practical links through projects etc. were more frequent on combined early years and junior courses than in the other three categories.

## 2.8 Changes in the courses

### 2.8.1 The National Curriculum

Question 13 asked what changes had occurred in the course in response to the introduction of the National Curriculum. The results are shown in Figure 2.8.1.

Figure 2.8.1 **Changes in courses because of National Curriculum (most frequently mentioned responses)**

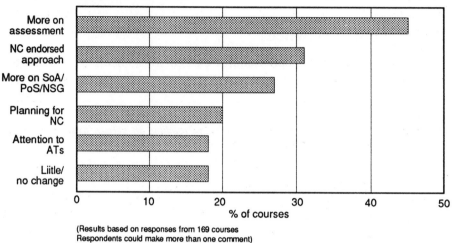

(Results based on responses from 169 courses
Respondents could make more than one comment)

Given the far-reaching changes brought about by the 1988 Education Act, it seems curious that even 18 per cent of respondents to this question reported 'little or no change'. The other items seem to show that course staff were addressing the problems.

### 2.8.2 Changes planned

Question 14 asked what changes were planned for the next two years: the results are given in Figure 2.8.2.

Figure 2.8.2 **Changes in courses in next two years (most frequently mentioned responses)**

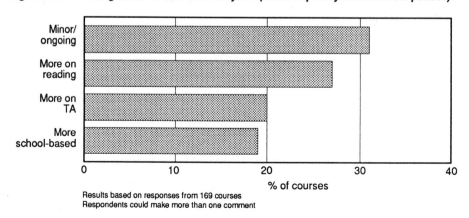

Results based on responses from 169 courses
Respondents could make more than one comment

36

The changes planned seem desirable even if not momentous. One feature of the data is that only the first of the four items in Figure 2.8.2 was mentioned by any respondent from a secondary course.

## 2.8.3 Changes wanted

The last item in the questionnaire to be reported here is question 15, which asked for the respondent's opinion on what the effect would be of amending the CATE criteria to require explicit courses in the teaching of reading: the results are presented in Figure 2.8.3.

**Figure 2.8.3** *Effects of amending CATE criteria (most frequently mentioned responses)*

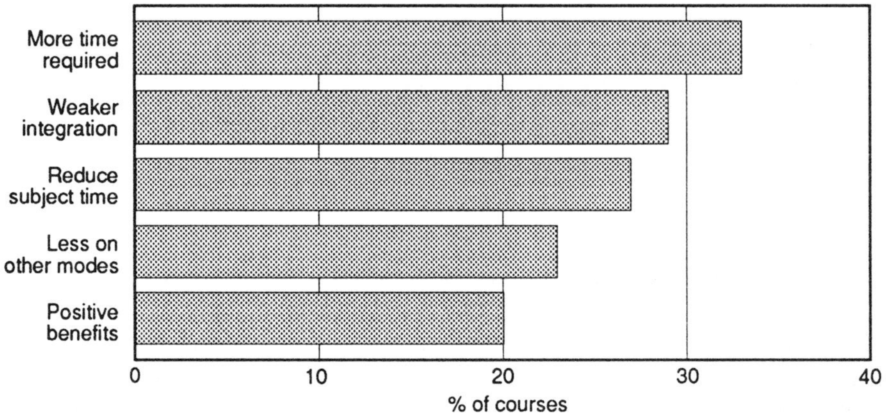

Results based on responses from i69 courses
Respondents could make more than one comment

Neither the second nor the third item was mentioned by any secondary respondents. The first item, however, chimes in with ideas expressed by staff during interviews. When asked what changes, if any, they would like to see in the CATE criteria, several said they would welcome more time for language and reading. They thought this should be achieved by altering the balance, on primary BEd courses at least, between subject specialisms and education studies: subject specialisms could be cut to, say, 40 per cent.

# Analysis of the Booklists

**by Alison Tate**

# ANALYSIS OF THE BOOKLISTS

As well as returning the questionnaire, institutions were asked to enclose other information about the teaching of reading on their courses, including the reading lists given to students. Reading lists were returned with 170 of the 181 institutional questionnaires. Not all of the 170 lists could be analysed in the time available, so exactly half (85) were coded and analysed. These 85 lists were selected randomly.

Across all courses, the range and variety of titles included in reading lists was notable. There were references to 718 different books, articles and reports. Only four titles were mentioned in more than 50 per cent of the reading lists; in all, 246 references occurred once each.

A previous study of reading course lists in initial teacher training in 1987-8 (Gorman, 1989) made the point that 'the majority of the books most frequently cited are not written to provide information about the initial teaching of reading. The exceptions are the texts by two New Zealanders, Clay and Holdaway, which attend in some detail to the question of how children might be assisted in learning about the relationships between printed and spoken language'. The present survey suggests that the situation has not changed significantly in this respect. No books dealing in any detail with the complex relationships between the writing system (the orthography) and the sound system (the phonology) of English, for example, are to be found among the 30 most common reference books, though Katherine Perera's book on *Children's Writing and Reading* deals with grammatical differences between speech and writing with insight.

The list includes the main current reports and guidance statements on reading. The high place on the list of the Bullock Report is of interest, although the somewhat lower frequency of mention of current guidance and reports is likely to relate to the fact that such documents are regarded as essential rather than optional reading. (This interpretation was confirmed by the interview data).

The overall list reflects attention to reading development over the primary and secondary age range and covers all stages of reading development. In general, one can note a practical, or applied, rather than theoretical bias. The list reflects the main areas of interest and developments in reading pedagogy over the last decade.

It covers the Schools Council's 'Effective Use of Reading' Project at the end of the 1970s, and its subsequent development of curriculum materials ('DARTS') (Lunzer and Gardner, 1979); apprenticeship methods and parental involvement (cf Waterland, 1985;1989; Tizard and Hughes, 1984); the influence of 'psycholinguistic' models of the reading process (Smith, 1978); the concern with the social context of literacy and pre-school language development (cf Wells, 1986); language diversity and the skills of bilingual pupils (cf Houlton, 1987); speech/written language relationships (Perera, 1984; Bryant and Bradley, 1982) and informal assessment and monitoring (Barrs, 1988). There is a notable absence of materials dealing with formal language assessment in a school context such as the reports of the APU Language Monitoring Team (cf. Gorman, 1986; White, 1986; Brooks, 1987; Gorman and Kispal, 1987; MacLure and Hargreaves, 1986; Gorman et al, 1991).

## Criteria for inclusion of references

The reading lists sent usually related to 'English' or 'Language and Literature' and were not always further subdivided. Where the list contained a specific section on reading, it was this that was coded.Otherwise, all references were included, leaving out only those books or articles primarily focusing on writing and spelling. This means that the lists of books given below cover both reading and related areas, including children's literature, literacy, sociolinguistics; language, psycholinguistics; bilingualism, etc.

Institutions were asked, in returning their booklists, to distinguish, if possible, between compulsory and recommended reading. For lists that were prioritised in this way, only books indicated as 'recommended' were coded. For lists that were not prioritised, all references were coded.

The 85 reading lists coded contained an average of 30 items. There were no major differences between PGCE and BEd courses in length, level, or content of the booklists. Far fewer lists were received from secondary courses, in line with their generally low response rate to the questionnaire on the teaching of reading.

In the lists below, the figure given in brackets after each item represents the percentage of reading lists analysed on which the item occurred.

## Table 3.1   Reading Lists: Overall Top Thirty Titles

1. WATERLAND, L. (1985). *Read With Me: an Apprenticeship Approach to Reading.* Stroud: Thimble Press,   (68%)

2. BEARD, R. (1987). *Developing Reading 3-13.* London: Hodder & Stoughton.   (57%)

3. MEEK, M. (1982). *Learning to Read.* London: Bodley Head   (54%)

4. SMITH, F. (1978). Reading. *Cambridge: Cambridge University* Press. 2nd edn 1985.   (52%)

5. HALL, N. (1987). *The Emergence of Literacy.* Sevenoaks: Hodder and Stoughton.   (45%)

6. BULLOCK REPORT. GREAT BRITAIN. DEPARTMENT OF EDUCATION AND SCIENCE (1975). *A Language for Life.* London: HMSO.   (42%)

7. MEEK, M. (Ed) (1988). *How Texts Teach what Readers Learn.* Stroud: Thimble Press.   (41%)

8. SOUTHGATE, V. *et al.* (1981). *Extending Beginning Reading.* London: Heinemann Educational for the Schools Council.   (39%)

9. ARNOLD, H. (1982). *Listening to Children Read.* London: Hodder & Stoughton.   (38%)

10. HOLDAWAY, D. (1979). *The Foundations of Literacy.* London: Ashton Scholastic.   (37%)

11. DES (1990). *English in the National Curriculum* (No.2). London: HMSO.   (34%)

12. MOON, C. (Ed.) (1985). *Practical Ways to Teach Reading.* London: Ward Lock Educational.   (34%)

13. WELLS, G. (1986). *The Meaning Makers: Children Learning Language and Using Language to Learn.* London: Hodder & Stoughton.   (32%)

14. HUTCHCROFT, D. (1981). *Making Language Work: a Practical Approach to Literacy for Teachers of 5- to 13-year old children.* Maidenhead: McGraw-Hill.   (27%)

15. BENNETT, J. (1982). *Learning to Read with Picture Books.* Stroud: Thimble Press.   (27%)

16. DES AND WELSH OFFICE (1989). *National Curriculum: English for Ages 5 to 16. Proposals of the Secretary of State for Education and Science and the Secretary of State for Wales* (The Cox Report). London: DES.   (24%)

17. LUNZER, E. and GARDNER, K. (1979). *The Effective Use of Reading.* London: Heinemann for the Schools Council.   (22%)

18. TIZARD, B. and HUGHES, M. (1984). *Young Children Learning: Talking and Thinking at Home and at School.* London: Fontana.   (21%)

19. WADE, B. (1990). *Reading for Real.* Milton Keynes: Open University Press.   (21%)

20. KINGMAN REPORT. GREAT BRITAIN. DEPARTMENT OF EDUCATION AND SCIENCE (1988). *Report of the Committee of Inquiry into the Teaching of English Language.* London: HMSO.   (20%)

21. HOULTON, D. (1987). *All Our Languages: a Handbook for the Multilingual Classroom.* London: Edward Arnold.   (20%)

22. MEEK, M. and MILLS, C. (Eds) (1988). *Language and Literacy in the Primary School.* London: Falmer Press.   (20%)

23. WATERLAND, L. (Ed) (1989). *Apprenticeship in Action: Teachers write about "Read With Me".* Stroud: Thimble Press   (20%)

24. BARRS, M. *et al.* (1988). *Patterns of Learning: The Primary Language Record and the Language Curriculum.* London: Centre for Language in Primary Education.   (20%)

25. WRAY, D. *et al.* (1989). *Literacy in Action.* London: Falmer Press.   (19%)

26. CLARK, M. (Ed) (1985). *New Directions in the Study of Reading.* London: Falmer Press.   (19%)

27. CLARK, M. (1979). *Reading Difficulties in Schools.* London: Heinemann.   (19%)

28. CLAY, M. (1979). *Reading: The Patterning of Complex Behaviour.* London: Heinemann.   (19%)

29. BRYANT, P. and BRADLEY, L. (1985). *Children's Reading Problems: Psychology and Education.* Oxford: Basil Blackwell.   (18%)

30. PERERA, K. (1984). *Children's Writing and Reading: Analysing Classroom Language.* Oxford: Basil Blackwell.   (18%)

# REFERENCES

BROOKS, G. (1987). *Speaking and Listening: Assessment at Age 15.*
Windsor: NFER-NELSON.

GORMAN, T.P. (1986). *The Framework for the Assessment of Language.*
Windsor, NFER/NELSON.

GORMAN, T.P. (1989). *What Teachers in Training Read about Reading,
Centre for Research in Language and Communication, Occasional
Paper 4.* Slough: NFER.

GORMAN, T.P. and KISPAL, A. (1987). *The Assessment of Reading.*
Windsor, NFER-NELSON.

GORMAN, T., WHITE, J., BROOKS, G. and ENGLISH F. (1991).
*Assessment Matters No.4. Language for Learning: a Summary
Report on the 1988 APU Language Monitoring Surveys.*
London: HMSO for SEAC and COI.

MacLURE, M. and HARGREAVES, M. (1986). *Speaking and Listening:
Assessment at Age 11.* Windsor: NFER-NELSON.

WHITE, J. (1986). *The Assessment of Writing: Pupils Aged 11 and 15.*
Windsor: NFER-NELSON.

The other titles cited are included in the booklist given in this paper.

# The Interview Data

**by Alison Tate**

# THE INTERVIEW DATA

## 4.1   The research design

### *4.1.1 The approach*

In order to provide a fuller picture of how courses dealt with reading, 20 of the 92 institutions with relevant courses were approached for permission to interview students and key staff.

The 20 institutions, and the courses within them, were selected to represent a range on each of the following factors

**Region**              Northern Ireland, Wales and, within England, the North, Midlands and South.

**Type of institution** Universities, polytechnics, and colleges or institutes of higher education.

**CATE district**       Not more than one institution from any CATE Local Committee - therefore only three CATE Districts were.unrepresented.

**Age-range**           Secondary and primary, and, within primary, junior and early years.
-   On this factor the interview sample was weighted towards primary and, within that, towards early years.

**Course type**         BEd or PGCE.
-   On this factor the sample was weighted towards BEd.

**Language**            In Wales, one course was selected which had both English- and Welsh-medium versions. In England, one course was selected which had a multilingual emphasis.

The weighting towards primary and BEd courses was due to our (justified) anticipation that less information on reading would be gathered from secondary and PGCE courses.

### 4.1.2    The samples

The interviews were carried out in two phases, eight institutions being visited in July and 12 in September/October. Key staff were interviewed in all 20 institutions. In addition, all the institutions were asked if it would be possible to interview a small group of students (not more than five). Because of the summer vacation, no students were available at any of the eight institutions visited in July. Also, at six of those visited in September/October no students were available whom it would have been relevant to interview (either they were already out on school experience or they would have been PGCE students in the first week of their course). Thus students were interviewed at six institutions: in all cases, those interviewed were fourth-year BEd students.

The numbers of people interviewed were:

Lecturers        52
Students        27.

The 20 courses from which lecturers were interviewed comprised:

Primary BEd                      12   (identified as A-K, and R)
Primary PGCE                      4   (identified as L-O)
Secondary PGCE and BEd     4   (identified as P, Q, S and T).

Interviewees were given the assurance that the resulting report would not identify institutions or individuals. Because of this, the institutions concerned are not identified.

As in the questionnaire, the main focus of the interviews was the aspects of teaching about reading that all students encountered on the course, rather than the preparation of English specialists. The interviews were semi-structured, following an interview schedule which had four main components relating to:

- information about the course

- the coverage of the reading in the course

- the school experience of students

- specialist aspects of the course.

The following commentary concentrates on the findings relating to primary courses, although some reference is made to secondary courses. The commentary focuses on the main issues that arose in the interviews.

## 4.2 The involvement of practising teachers in planning, evaluating and teaching courses (secondary and primary courses)

### 4.2.1 Lecturing

One of the questions asked in the interviews was about the involvement of practising teachers in the taught parts of the course; teachers, of course, were always heavily involved in students' school experience.

Two courses reported that there was no involvement of practising teachers in their course (one primary B.Ed (F); one secondary BEd (S)). There were only four instances of teachers being involved in the planning or evaluation of the course (F; G; O; R), although a fifth course referred to a local consortium of teachers who played a large part in all aspects of the degree, and this involvement may have included planning and evaluation.

Secondment of teachers was referred to (C; E). But it was clear that teachers were involved most often as speakers or in running sessions on particular topics (D; H; G; J; K; L; M). The areas most frequently mentioned were special needs or dyslexia (H; M; Q) and assessment, particularly in relation to SATs. Other instances mentioned were:

- the Language Co-ordinator from a local primary school coming in to talk about planning a language policy (J)

- early writing (L)

- a local teacher who was also a writer of early literacy texts as guest speaker (Q).

A number of courses devoted a specific block of time to preparation of English specialist students for a language advisory or curriculum leadership role, and such options often involved guest speakers, including practising teachers (H; Q; M).

### 4.2.2 Other kinds of involvement

There was a variety of other kinds of teacher involvement. In two instances, links with local teachers were used at the beginning of PGCE courses to introduce students to the perspective of practising teachers. On one secondary PGCE, local teachers had co-authored the briefing booklet given to students before an initial placement in primary schools (P). A primary PGCE (M) used a panel of local heads to brief students in groups before they began an initial three-week placement at the beginning of the course, and to debrief the students after their placement. This was a scheme which was reported as having run successfully for a number of years. It was suggested that the local heads, for whom the time commitment was of the order of two to three days, saw their input as part of their professional responsibilities. A sense of 'ownership' had clearly developed, the group selecting its own new members if individuals dropped out. One college was operating a partnership 'conferencing' programme in which teachers, students and supervisors took part in round-table discussions in schools. This college had also started a telephone canvassing system: phoning a small number of headteachers to establish practitioners' views on current issues (C).

### 4.2.3 Limitations on teacher involvement

Most interviewees were positive about extending teacher involvement in aspects of the course, but recognised problems in doing this. Funding was felt to be a limitation. In one course (C), INSET funding, which had now come to an end, had supported a programme of teacher involvement that students described warmly. Class teachers, and in some cases headteachers, were able to visit the college on a regular basis to consider with students the kind of reading practices they had seen in schools. If the funding were to be available, the college would be keen to repeat the activity, but would want to use it later in the students' programme.

There was an instance of local teachers being used as 'teacher-tutors', not for students, but for staff. The scheme involved continuing links between staff teaching on the course, and specific teachers in the locality; these teachers were sometimes involved in teaching on the degree. In this instance, payment was involved, at least for the teaching input, and it was suggested that the limited sum available restricted the teacher-tutors' involvement (L).

Two interviewees were using or developing schemes whereby lecturers took the place of classroom teachers for occasional days, freeing teachers to work with students in college (I).

Other problems mentioned were teachers' lack of professional expertise, and restrictions imposed by the institution's Academic Board in degree assessment.

## 4.3 Approaches to early reading (primary courses)

### *4.3.1 General*

The primary BEd and primary PGCE interview data provide a useful illustration of courses' approaches to early reading, as well as a rationale for the approaches chosen. The supplementary course documentation provided by various courses will also be referred to in this section. Since 'the reading debate' has been a focus of attention for some time now, this material included a number of examples of institutions' or courses' 'position statements' on reading policy, sometimes prepared for students, in other cases as Select Committee evidence or in connection with HMI inspections and surveys.

The interviews revealed a striking consensus among courses concerned with the teaching of early reading: interviewees stressed the need for an 'integrated' approach to language skills, and 'eclecticism' in the choice of teaching strategies. There was no apparent difference between BEd courses and PGCE courses in this respect. This high degree of consensus was also reflected in the additional course documentation forwarded with the questionnaires.

There were striking similarities also in course content and methodology, which is perhaps not surprising, given the degree to which courses are tightly controlled by the CATE criteria. The dimensions on which courses vary are discussed below; overall the similarities were more striking. Before discussing in detail what, precisely, was meant by 'integration' and 'eclecticism' in approaches to early reading, there are three general points, derived from the range of interviews, that it may be useful to make about courses' approach to training students to teach reading.

### i) A commitment to active teaching of reading

No interviewee suggested that reading skills were likely to be 'caught' rather than taught, or that children were likely to acquire reading skills without specific help and intervention by the teacher. One interviewee expressed her view as follows:

'In terms of cognition, reading is an applied cognitive act rather than a natural one, and so it has to be taught rather than being allowed to develop spontaneously'. Or, as it was put in a position statement, in this case from one institution's course documentation:

*Most emphatically we do **not** believe that teaching children to read is just a matter of liberating children by, as it were, throwing them into a swimming pool of lovely books in which they are invited to wallow. If children are not given human support and armbands, and taught a stroke or two, they may be submerged.*

All course staff interviewed envisaged active intervention by the teacher in teaching children to read. This intervention included employing a range of specific activities and strategies in the teaching of reading and the provision and use of carefully chosen materials, as well as management of the 'literacy environment' of the classroom.

## ii) Severe time constraints

Course coverage of initial reading serves only to introduce issues and teaching strategies to students. Because of pressure on courses in terms of their coverage, the amount of time that can be spent on any one topic or area is severely limited. It appeared quite common, for instance, for the main treatment of 'phonics' or of reading schemes to take place within one or two lectures and associated tutorials or workshop sessions.

One example may give an indication of this necessarily broad    coverage.  It is one primary PGCE's informal listing of topics covered in the taught curriculum during the first term.  These were:

- language/dialect
- the terminology of primary English (KAL: what are children likely to do what children need to know; grammar and punctuation)
- language development and acquisition (e.g. videos of young children talking)
- reading in the National Curriculum
- approaches to teaching reading
- reading research; hearing children read; organising resources programmes of study; shared/paired reading.

This was the 'reading block' of lectures, which was followed by  similar coverage relating to writing and oracy.  The term's work also included drama. Timetabling pressures meant that IT and English were covered in lunchtime sessions.

Two points emerge. Interviewees felt that the timetabled 'reading' elements of the course considerably underestimated the extent to which 'reading' figured in the course.  They stressed that this scheduled attention to reading represented only the tip of an iceberg, in that these course elements were reinforced for students by practical activities and school experience and through the revisiting of topics when learning about associated areas.  In effect this means that to understand how 'reading' figures in a particular course, one has to pay considerable attention to the way lectures, assignments and school experience are integrated.

Yet interviewees were also aware of the introductory and limited nature of their coverage of the teaching of reading. The point was made several times in interviews. One lecturer interviewed, for example, pointed out that, if a student happened to miss one session in a course of lectures or seminars, this could result in an enormous gap in his or her knowledge (J). In relation to a different course, one student commented: 'It's so jam-packed that if you miss it, you miss it, there's no going back' (S).

The point was made several times in interviews (A; J). In one, staff expressed the hope that students recognised that what they received in training was just an initial course to prepare them for their probationary year, and that they actually needed more training (J). In another institution, it was reported that the course's own student evaluation had made the staff aware that many students found this area of professional expertise (i.e. reading) a difficult one; lecturers stressed that skills in the teaching of reading needed to be systematically developed over the first years of a teaching career (L).

### iii) A practical focus and a little theoretical underpinning

Courses were not taught at a theoretical level: they were practical and activity-focused. One interviewee pointed out that reading and cognitive development, for example, was 'just touched upon in most B.Ed courses as a little theoretical underpinning', although it was covered in depth by English specialists on the same course (J). Other theoretical perspectives, if they were referred to in courses, appeared to fulfil a similar role as minimal theoretical underpinning. This assessment is supported by the analysis of the course reading lists, in which once again one finds a notably practical rather than theoretical bias. One interviewee described such an approach as learning the teaching of reading by teaching rather than by theory (Q), another as having the objective that students should be able to 'defend' any particular or general approach to reading that they chose to adopt (I).

### 4.3.2 The integration of language skills

Most courses emphasised the need for an integrated, holistic (F; I) or 'whole language' (C) approach to the development of children's language skills. What did this mean in practice? It was certainly not the case that the reading elements of the courses were unidentifiable. The most common pattern was of a block of lectures/ workshops on reading followed by a similar block on writing and on oracy (a pattern occasionally reversed, on the grounds of a more natural developmental sequence). 'Integration', in the courses discussed in interviews, seemed to have two associated characteristics.

- Children's early reading was discussed in the context of 'emergent literacy' (in addition to any other theoretical influences in the presentation of 'reading' which might be introduced). In one institution 'emergent literacy' was glossed as 'the placing of literacy culturally and socially, looking at relationships between home and school'. Commonly, then, courses presented reading in relation to the early acquisition of language, work on the social context of the development of children's oral skills and the relationship between home and school language.

- Children's reading and writing were therefore presented as closely linked. One institution, for example, suggested that students learned much about children's reading by looking at their writing, i.e. identifying the influences, models and generic influences in the writing and considering how such analyses might be used to suggest ways of helping a child extend his or her reading repertoire (F). Other examples of the close link between reading and writing were: reinforcing awareness of phonics by attention to children's spelling strategies (H); using reading as a stimulus for speaking and/or writing tasks (M); making links between writing, drama, oracy and reading; and the use of IT programmes to develop children's reading and writing skills (H; M).

### 4.3.3 The eclectic approach

As one interviewee commented (L), 'eclecticism rules' in regard to the methods of teaching reading that courses covered. Eclecticism, in this case, was variously explained as the attempt to describe and exemplify all models of teaching reading to students (L), or as a stress on the combination of approaches so that different approaches to reading were seen as complementary rather than mutually exclusive (B). There was a broad similarity among the rationales put forward for the adoption of such a policy. Firstly, it was suggested, it follows current recommendations, that is, advice from HMI and the statutory and nonstatutory Guidance on English in the National Curriculum. Secondly, it was argued that such a policy is supported by current research findings. Some of the individual points put forward by interviewees are listed below:

- any single approach ran the danger of making 'blanket assumptions' about children (F)

- eclecticism was a response to the diversity of children in schools, especially since Warnock (H)

- there was no answer to the problems of teaching reading inherent in any single approach (F)

- there was a need for individual approaches to suit the needs of individual children (H)

- no one method works with every child (K)
- teachers need a variety of techniques at their disposal (B; J).

The stress, as will be apparent, was on the choice of teaching strategies to suit the learning strategies and problems of individual children.

One instance where there appeared to be some difference between courses was in the area of how prescriptively they advocated an eclectic approach to students. Two courses (B; M) - both primary PGCEs - stressed that they were not prescriptive, i.e. they preferred to point out differences, advantages and disadvantages of different methods but let students make up their own minds.

An issue that was raised twice in interviews was the extent to which students were confused by the range of approaches and methodologies they encountered. A student interviewed commented that 'It would be nice to have a structure to implement' (K). One PGCE course (B) felt that students often were initially confused but in time began to perceive a 'coherent whole'. A lecturer on a BEd course felt that some but not all of the Year 4 students 'would be able to say, at the end of their course, how it all fitted together' (J). It was also pointed out that students' knowledge of and allegiance to different methods were affected by their school placements. Staff at J pointed out that students' knowledge and experience of teaching methods varied according to the schools they happened to practise in, and that they were very influenced by the teaching practices that they saw used at first hand.

### 4.3.4 Phonics within an eclectic approach

Phonics featured in all courses, according to the staff interviewed.Students, in one case, were unsure. Two courses stressed that they gave 'technical instruction' (G) in the use of phonics; in one case this was directly related to working within a bilingual context. Interviewees tended to stress their view of phonics not as a technique, or as the basis for a reading programme, but rather as one strategy of attack: one kind of 'cue' among a range of semantic and contextual cues that readers need to be able to use (D; E). As such, phonics were regarded as 'indispensable - part of the skills that children need in becoming readers' (B). Phonic games and materials featured in most of the courses' resources centres that were visited.

The general point to stress, perhaps, is that phonics were regarded as important, but, as the sole approach to the teaching of reading, inadequate. Encouraging children to use other cues or strategies, such as word recognition, and paying attention to visual cues such as pictures or illustrations, were felt to be equally important. Interviewees tended to play down any idea of incompatibility betweenhelping children to use phonic cues in early reading and 'reading for meaning'.

Correspondingly, the idea of treating phonic approaches as the main or sole strategy of intervention open to teachers was regarded with suspicion. In one interview (H), for example, staff made the following points about an over-reliance or sole reliance on phonic methods:

- that there was a danger of 'mechanistic' approaches being employed, particularly with insecure teachers

- some phonic programmes took responsibility from the teacher

- over-attention to phonics involved the danger that other aspects of reading might be marginalised.

It is not the case that students were thoroughly prepared for the teaching of phonics; but neither, of course, were they prepared thoroughly for the teaching of any other approach. We interviewed a student who was 'still not sure how to use books as real books'. The point that teacher training courses can only offer an introduction to various strategies of teaching reading was one that was repeatedly emphasised by those interviewed.

### 4.3.5 Reading schemes and real books

There was a large degree of consensus apparent in the way the courses treated reading schemes and kits, described in one case as 'range and variety' (C). All provided the opportunity for students to discuss or evaluate a range of reading schemes. In many cases courses had their own collection of readers, covering in one case at least, a historical range from *Janet and John* to the newer story kits (M).

Courses tended not to advocate particular reading schemes. Most said they did not recommend any specific schemes to students, although on two courses *Ginn 360* was dealt with in detail because of its popularity in local schools (D; M) and, on another, *Story Chest* was a focus (L). Student assignments and school-based projects were sometimes linked to a review of reading schemes (M; F).

Only one course declared a bias towards 'real books' (Q), although in at least one other course, students felt that this was an implicit bias. In fact, the term 'real books' was not often used in interviews; in one case it was stressed that real books were 'not a panacea' (G); in another, that they were a 'resource not a method' (D). This was indicative of the fact that few interviewees appeared to feel that there was any necessary opposition between the use of reading schemes and of 'real books' in the classroom. A degree of exasperation towards the tenor of the current debate about reading, and what was regarded as its unnecessary and unhelpful polarisation of approaches, was often apparent.

Interviewees' attitudes to this question perhaps can be better understood in relation to their commitment to the use of story and literature in the classroom, and to their views on reading development. Most courses placed great stress on familiarising students with the range of children's literature, poetry and drama. This is, of course, entirely in line with National Curriculum recommendations, and, indeed, one interviewee commented that the National Curriculum was very supportive of using 'story' as a starting point in developing children's reading.

The concern with story and literature, evident in both early and junior years primary courses, is related to the expressed objectives and aims of courses in relation to reading. Most staff interviewees stressed their course's concern not only with teaching children to read but helping children to become 'readers', to read for pleasure and interest (F), to become 'fluent and competent readers' (J), increasing their voluntary reading as well as their ability to read (Q; F).

This is an objective that addresses a specific problem, long identified in the teaching of reading, i.e. the problem summarised by staff on one course (F) as follows: 'A lot of children do not enjoy reading and find it very painful. Most children learn to read but few choose to read for pleasure.' The main justification of 'real books' approaches, i.e. the use of non-simplified quality reading books in the classroom, is that they are more likely to encourage children to enjoy reading or become 'readers'.

A point to note, is that, in general, lecturers do not make, and do not encourage students to make, a division between teaching children the skills and strategies needed to decipher text and developing the attitudes and skills characteristic of fluent and enthusiastic readers. These two objectives of the teaching of reading are not regarded as divisible, nor as chronologically sequenced (i.e. a first stage in which children learn to decode text and a second in which they become interested and self-motivated readers). The argument here would be that no matter how effective 'mechanistic' decoding strategies (e.g. drills; decontextualised exercises; learning of phonic rules) might be, they would not persuade children that reading material, literary or non-literary, can be rewarding, informative, useful or exciting. An additional argument would be that, in any case, there is no evidence that such methods necessarily produce competent readers; they appear to work with some children, but fail with others.

Several courses had discussed the ongoing debate with their students. It is of interest that a number of courses commented ruefully that the reading scheme/ real books debate was echoed among students; in one case this was said to lead occasionally to violent arguments, with protagonists dividing into 'real books' and 'reading scheme' camps (M).

## 4.4 Classroom organisation

### 4.4.1 Background

The interviews indicated that the use of the term 'classroom organisation' raised problems of interpretation. Since the issue of classroom organisation is generic on teacher training courses, in a number of interviews the initial reaction to a question on this area was to point out that classroom organisation was handled in other parts of the course (D; H; M; Q). In most cases, later questions revealed that aspects of classroom organisation of reading were, in fact, given considerable attention on the course concerned.

The problem relates to the fact that a broad definition of classroom organisation can potentially cover every aspect of teaching reading: for example, on one course it was stressed that among the 'easier' competencies that the course aimed to develop in students were: being able to organise reading in the classroom; being able to assess the needs of individual children; being competent in a range of strategies to meet difficulties; being able to work with other people, making maximum use of helpers and aids (F). Potentially, all these competencies involve classroom organisation. In another interview, it was stressed that the issue of organisation was fundamental to teaching practice, too: this was the area of experience where students had to learn how to organise their teaching time and the children's reading time, and cope with the management of stress (J).

Since the recent HMI report on the teaching of reading in schools identified classroom organisation as one of the most problematic areas for teachers, it is perhaps worth stressing that the term needs 'unpacking' if it is to be useful. In the interviews, other phrases such as 'organising group work', 'managing the learning environment', 'managing resources' and 'managing the language curriculum', though not necessarily more precise, did trigger rather more focused responses.

### 4.4.2 Definitions and practices

The range of points mentioned in response to the question about classroom organisation in interviews demonstrates the range of meanings the term can have. But, despite problems of nomenclature, courses clearly varied in respect to which aspects of classroom management were given explicit attention and how these were handled. The following aspects of classroom organisation were stressed:

- **Classroom organisation as curriculum planning**, for example in terms of 'finding space and time for reading in a busy primary classroom' (L). Staff in one institution felt that this was a particular problem in later primary teaching, when 'reading' ceased to figure on the timetable (D).

- **Classroom organisation as the physical organisation** of the classroom (B; M). Staff at one institution organised model 'layouts' in their Resources Centre (D); staff at another pointed out that the disposition of both the classroom and the pupils within it was one of the aspects students had to include in their detailed lesson plans on teaching practice (M).

- **Students' experience with group work**, and, more broadly, staging students' experience in working with pupils. It was relatively common on serial school experience visits for students first to work with an individual child, then with a group of children and to move on to take responsibility for the whole class for a limited session (e.g. in introducing, reading or telling a story). Yet there were divergences in the amount of attention given to this issue. One PGCE course reported that organisation of group work was an issue that arose most obviously in relation to oracy work, although it intermittently figured in relation to reading. Another referred to a number of sessions on organising group work using different management strategies. There was considerable attention to the currently popular procedures expressed in the acronyms DEAR, USSR, etc. One PGCE gave particular attention to hearing groups of pupils, as well as individual pupils, read.

- **Managing resources.** Attention to the organisation of resources within the classroom was mentioned in several interviews: the arrangement of book corners and the like. More generally, the importance of managing the learning environment was sometimes stressed, for example, the issue of 'how you create a stimulating language environment' (F). A lecturer on another course described how it mounted a series of exhibitions and displays concentrating on three or four of the National Curriculum attainment targets for English, and related books and materials (L).

- **Modelling**: trying to ensure that the lectures, workshops and demonstrations within the taught parts of the course demonstrated a variety of modes of organisation which students could evaluate and employ.

A number of interviewees - staff and students - pointed out that work on classroom organisation was best done in the classroom. In initial school placements (particularly in the one- to three-week placements that were characteristically located at the beginning of PGCE courses), the observation of the teacher's classroom management strategies was suggested as an area to which students should pay attention. Staff on one course (L) pointed out, however, that organisational issues did not mean a lot to students until they had had a chance to 'do it themselves'. In this course, it was suggested, issues of classroom management were handled predominantly through tutoring in schools.

(Students had the same tutors for school and institutional aspects of their course.) Staff also felt that the organisation of students into small tutor groups was important in allowing students a chance to talk through the problems they encountered in schools.

## 4.5  Developing reading

Developing reading was a concern of teacher training courses across the age range. A clear demarcation between developing reading in relation to fiction and non-fiction was apparent. The former was discussed in relation to the use of story and narrative in the classroom and, more generally, in the context of children's literature. The second tended to be discussed in terms of study and information retrieval skills.

### 4.5.1 Story and literature (primary courses)

Staff on most primary courses, whether focusing on early years or junior years, placed considerable stress on the use of stories and literature in the classroom. This area was occasionally an option (F), but more often an obligatory element of the course.

Interviewees pointed out that one important way of developing children's reading was through children's literature (H; B) and that, broadly speaking, the National Curriculum was very supportive of literature as a starting point (F). The development of students' appreciation of literature was considered important in itself, i.e. helping students respond to and learn more about literature (B; F). Courses included, variously, sessions on:

- Inviting students to look at strategies of challenging and extending children's reading (F).

- Work on children's attitudes to reading: how children approach books (B).

- Using literature as a basis for role play (F), and drama activities as a stimulus for writing (M).

- Children's literature as a basis for topic work (M).

- Literature and personal and social development - e.g. with reference to the novels of Judy Blume (M).

- Reading to children (including voice projection skills) (M).

- A story-telling workshop including a professional story- teller (L).

- Guidance for students on a range of children's literature (L); choosing books for children (M). That the main review journals often featured on booklists is evidence of a shared concern on this issue. Several courses emphasised reviewing materials for gender bias or mono-cultural bias (B; D; F). One interviewee commented that this kind of activity 'currently engages students, students are very conscious of these issues' (D).

Examples of tasks given as assignments or tasks set in visits to schools (i.e. serial school experience) included:

- Production of 'Big Books' for use in classrooms (C; M).

- Students being asked to make a text for a child in the first term of the language course, and in their second term to make a book for a child and write a brief commentary on the process of compiling it. This involves research into books for children as well as talking with children about their reading tastes (F).

- Simplifying a non-literary text for children aged two years younger than the readability level of the original (J: English specialism).

- The selection and use in the classroom of a particular book for children. Students have to demonstrate their classroom introduction of the book to other students and produce a written review (L).

- The organisation and display of children's books in a classroom book area (L).

### 4.5.2 Non-literary texts

All courses included some attention to ways of developing children's non-literary reading. This tended to include:

- introducing students to specific ways of looking closely at texts (F)
- consideration of what teachers need to do to get children to interrogate books (L)
- using dictionaries (M)
- locating and using information (M)
- skimming and scanning (F)
- links with topic work (M)
- reading kits and SRA (M)
- fast reading strategies (M)
- comprehension strategies (L)
- DARTS (most courses)
- cloze procedure (F; L)
- sequencing (F)
- work on genres (L).

An overview of comments on the introduction of these kinds of activities to students is informative: there were complaints about the lack of suitable non-literary texts for early readers (J). Two course tutors commented that they tried to use materials from schools for this kind of work (D; M). A further point made related to the value of workshops in this area, of getting students not just to do exercises but also to raise questions as a result (L), i.e. stressing a critical approach to information texts; the phrase 'interrogating texts' was used by several interviewees in this context. Another course tutor felt that it was important that such activities were contextualised, not just treated as isolated exercises on fragments of texts (F).

## 4.6   Knowledge about language (primary courses)

One area in which there was considerable variation among courses was in the extent to which they felt it was desirable that students should be introduced to any formal knowledge about language, and if so, of what kind. Both the interviews and the relatively prominent position of the Kingman Report on the booklist survey indicate that the role of linguistics in the teaching of reading is still a live issue which gives rise to debate and disagreement. It should be said that the interview data may be skewed by the fact that the interviewees were not always those individuals responsible for the linguistics input to the course.

### 4.6.1 *Coverage*

It may be useful to raise initially the question of what courses covered in relation to 'knowledge about language' (KAL). The following list represents a composite picture drawn from interviews across primary courses.

- Some coverage of issues relating to language diversity, particularly in relation to regional dialects and accents, and also covering the position of Standard English. In some courses, attention was also given to ethnic variation, ESOL and bilingualism. Language variation over time was not a topic that was mentioned in many interviews, although it may be dealt with elsewhere on courses, for example in relation to children's literature.

- Language development and acquisition. This tended to involve teaching about the nature of spoken language, a focus on the development of children's language, early literacy, interactional patterns at home and school and differences between writing and speech. There was little evidence of any in-depth coverage of phonetics, an area sometimes argued to be a necessary underpinning to teaching phonic strategies. However, one course tutor explained that its teaching about phonics was grounded in the study of the orthographic and sound systems of English.

- The National Curriculum requirements and recommendations concerning KAL; the terminology used with reference to the primary English curriculum.

- Grammar: in interviews, questions about the treatment of grammar on courses indicated considerable variation among courses in approach and sophistication. Minimally, 'grammar' might entail a discussion of National Curriculum requirements and an introduction to 'parts of speech' - nouns, verbs, adjectives etc. Sometimes 'grammar, spelling and punctuation' were grouped together (M).

Elsewhere the approach was more linguistically oriented. In one BEd course, for example, language was presented as 'a number of different systems operating at different levels' (H). Some courses included a brief introduction to sentence structure. Crystal (J) and Quirk (H) were the only linguistics texts referred to; there were one or two references to functional grammatical models (e.g. Halliday) but mainly in relationship to early child development. In relation to this issue, it is of interest that no introductory linguistics texts featured at all highly in the book list analysis. Several courses stressed their applied focus; work on sentence structure was often associated with the examination of children's writing, sometimes with the study of the difficulty of reading materials.

- Text structure: there were several references to work on text structure (i.e. discourse above sentence level or narrative structure) which, again, was often approached through the discussion of children's writing, or through analysis of other texts, e.g. media texts or story structure. Research on the structure of oral interaction was referred to (e.g. on classroom interaction). Work on developing children's non-literary reading, such as DARTS, was sometimes suggested to be of value in relation to the structure of written texts (e.g. I). There were three references to current work on 'genre'.

Work on texts was often linked to an emphasis on developing students' critical skills. Lecturers on one course (D), for example, stressed their concern to emphasise not just chunks of text but 'whole texts', explaining that this derived from their overall view of language. Tutors on another course (F) stressed that their lectures focused on the understanding of the grammar of texts large and small, and aimed at increasing students' understanding of the structures of texts produced. They spent a lot of time looking at children's writing and at ways of helping children to become more capable writers. Work in this area tended to overlap with some of the kinds of text analysis discussed above under the heading *Developing reading*.

A few courses appeared to include some attention to language or textstructure in specialist subject studies other than English (e.g. language in science; language in maths) although further enquiry would be necessary to determine the extent of this. It is, incidentally, of interest that there were indications of wide divergences in the explicit attention to knowledge about language in the preparation of English specialists. From the interview data, for most BEd students, any such grounding appears to depend on whether linguistics is covered in their subject degree study of English, or not. For PGCE English specialist students, similarly, any thorough formal grounding in language derives from their earlier degree studies.

## 4.6.2 Problems

There are three general points that should be noted about courses' treatment of knowledge about language.

### i) Time constraints

Even if an explicit grounding in aspects of language structure - phonetics, syntax or discourse - were to be considered desirable, it is hard to see how time could be found for any extended treatment of these areas of study in either BEd or PGCE courses, given the range of current requirements to be fulfilled by such courses.

While questions about KAL produced references to a wide range of topics and activities, in most cases the treatment of these was of an introductory nature only, at best serving the purpose of consciousness-raising or of 'mapping' the area for students. This point was made forcefully in one interview in relation to a course which did attempt to introduce students to linguistics. The interviewees pointed out that one hour a week on language for the average BEd student was not enough; there was not enough time to cover much ground with most students about either language development or knowledge about language. In relation to another primary BEd (H), it was pointed out that the introduction to grammar that the course provided was limited but the course couldn't 'do everything'; it was suggested that they had, in fact, done more before the current time allocations for subject areas were introduced. The staff interviewed stressed the need for in-service training to 'pick up' on this area.

### ii) The difficulties of presenting a complex area to students

In several interviews, there were indications of the difficulty of presenting any formal models of language to students. One lecturer (J) commented that in recent years it had been found that trainees were arriving without the metalanguage necessary for talking about language. One of the problems was, therefore, that of providing them with this knowledge. Students, it was felt, needed a very simple introduction to linguistics which they could use straightaway and apply to children's writing. This view was echoed in another interview (B) where staff stressed that their students tended not to have much formal knowledge of language structure, although they often had rich language backgrounds. This was one of the reasons why the course did not attempt to introduce students to formal work on grammar.

There were suggestions that perhaps the primary aim of teaching students about language was to emphasise the importance of language in education to students; this was not something that they would necessarily be aware of. One course (J) commented that their infant/nursery practitioners were most exposed to the 'centrality of language' and were aware of oral language and its interconnectedness with reading and writing. Primary students, on the other hand, had to be 'made aware of their own ignorance' (and 'frightened into reading David Crystal's introductory linguistics book').

### iii)   Formal presentation of language to students was not always considered necessary or appropriate

Whatever the difficulties of language education for students, there was also clear evidence of a divergence among courses on the value of a formal or explicit introduction to language. There were those who felt this was not either necessary or desirable, and others who held it to be important.

Comments from three interviews can be used to illustrate the first position. In relation to one PGCE course (L), staff commented that knowledge about language was acquired *en passant* by students. They made no attempt to teach formal structures; nearly all their students had done French or some other modern language which provided them with a basic knowledge of grammar. Staff felt that some knowledge about language was useful for talking about writing but doubted it was necessary beyond this. On another course, it was explained that most of the course team were not convinced about whether there was a close relationship between an explicit ability to describe language and an ability to use it effectively. In another institution, lecturers were equally critical of the idea of any explicit teaching of language: it was not desirable to have theory separated from classroom activities. KAL, they felt, fed into or permeated all their courses.

## 4.6.3   LINC

Inevitably, given the timing of the interviews, the decision by the DES not to sponsor the publication of the LINC project's materials was an issue raised in many interviews. Some course tutors had developed quite close contacts with regional LINC coordinators, particularly in relation to their English specialism (e.g. H); others appeared to have little information about the project. All who raised the issue regretted the non-availability of LINC materials. Even interviewees who argued against the formal or explicit teaching of language to students in teacher training courses would have liked, at least, to have tried out the in-service materials developed by this project (e.g. L).

## 4.6.4 Bilingualism

There was a wide range of variation between courses in relation to the extent to which they explicitly addressed the issue of teaching reading to children from a range of language backgrounds. There was also considerable variety in the extent to which interviewees appeared to feel that this was an important issue, or one that they had expected to be raised in relation to reading. In relation to three primary courses, interviewees commented that they did not feel their course gave bilingualism much attention (E; I; M).

Overall, it appeared that there were four main ways in which bilingual and multilingual issues were raised in relation to the taught parts of courses.

- 'Multiculturalism' was often referred to as being handled in other parts of courses, for example as part of 'core themes' or in the context of equal opportunities (E; K; M). Not all interviewees saw any necessary link between multiculturalism and reading.

- Most courses referred to bilingualism in the context of a more general introduction to language diversity and the range and value of children's existing language experience. This was sometimes reinforced by additional sessions specifically on bilingualism (G; I; R).

- Some courses made special reference to multicultural children's literature (E; F; M), e.g. the use of 'parallel texts' on an infant/junior course.

- As already noted, many courses included sessions where students reviewed bias and cultural stereotyping in literary and non-literary works (although the main focus of this kind of analysis appeared to be gender rather than ethnicity).

There seemed to be two factors accounting for the wide divergence in practice between courses in the attention that they gave to bilingual issues. One was the ethnic composition of the area where the institution was located. One course explained its relative lack of attention to bilingual issues on the grounds that this was a teaching situation that its students were unlikely to face.

In contrast, in Wales (as the officially bilingual region of southern Britain), or in courses with a multilingual remit, bilingualism was regarded as having important implications for the teaching of reading as for every other area of the curriculum. One such course referred to itself as working within a 'context of bilingualism'. On some courses, and only on these courses, it appeared that issues relating to bilingualism were linked explicitly to the treatment of knowledge about language. Students were expected to have sufficient familiarity with the main community language(s) to allow them, for example, to identify language interference as a possible source of difficulties in children's reading. They were also expected to understand something of the debates on the nature of second language acquisition.

But the location of the institution was not the only factor affecting courses' attention to bilingualism. One rurally based college addressed the issues directly by what was referred to as a 'takeover' of a London school by its Year 3 students for three weeks each year (a scheme that had been functioning successfully for around ten years).

Courses that were particularly concerned with this area tended to

- arrange day or part-day visits to particular schools. For example, one BEd course systematically used a local school which was regarded as having excellent multiracial policies as the focus of its visits (H). Some courses clearly went to considerable trouble to arrange visits to areas some distance away - to a nursery in Bradford, for example (H).

- ensure that at least one teaching practice took place in multilingual schools (e.g. L; R).

## 4.7 Diagnosis and assessment, monitoring and record-keeping (primary courses)

### 4.7.1 *Issues*

The questionnaire data raised questions about the extent to which courses carry their emphasis on teachers using a variety of strategies in teaching reading through to stressing diagnosis of problems and the planning of suitable work for individual children. Ensuring variety and progression for all individuals in a class of 30 or more children challenges teachers' skills of assessment, monitoring and record-keeping. Did lecturers appear to identify this issue as a problem area, and if so, what techniques, guidelines or formats did they introduce students to?

Broad tendencies were apparent. Informal modes of assessment were stressed. Much attention was paid to 'hearing children read' (although one course (D) doubted the value of the practice and felt it needed 'unpacking'), and to reading conferences (A; B; C; D) for their diagnostic and monitoring value. Miscue analysis was mentioned by almost every course (A; B; C; D; I; J; K; L) although one interviewee doubted if sufficient time was given to it 'to make it work for the students'.

Equal attention was paid to methods of profiling, the keeping of running records and the use of various other instruments which function both as diagnostic, monitoring and record-keeping devices. Sometimes local or LEA frameworks were referred to (A). The Primary Language Record (recommended in the Cox report) was frequently mentioned (A; K; L; O), in one case as 'theoretically sound' and 'wonderfully pure' but as needing some modification for use in the classroom (L).

The only mention of reading schemes as representing an approach to monitoring progression, or as helpful in identifying a child's stage of reading development came from a student ('the easy way out') (A). The National Curriculum Statements of Attainment were not referred to as useful for diagnostic purposes, although staff on one course (F) asked their first-year students to plot an individual child's level against the relevant Reading SoAs. Another held a session familiarising students with the sequencing and development of reading levels embodied in the National Curriculum AT for reading (M). The NC and the Programmes of Study were, of course, a constant source of reference in other respects and it was generally felt to be extremely important that students should be familiar with them.

### 4.7.2 Examples

In interviews it was occasionally pointed out to us that in the area of planning, monitoring and record-keeping, the issue was one of providing structured experience for students rather than 'lectures' (A). The following are examples of tasks or projects set during, or closely related to, school experience sessions.

- Observation tasks, often structured by a task outline or by checklists to be completed (F). Judging by student comments, they appreciated the experience of watching teachers use different approaches, e.g. reading conferences, watching groups of children 'reading with leaders', paired reading, USSR. Such examples were referred to far more often in interviews than were lectures.

- Assessing one child's reading level, and recording evidence of problems, preferences and abilities.

- Studying a group of children. For example, in one course (G), students in Year 1 had the assignment of identifying children of different abilities in reading and working with them over a number of visits, the work resulting in a seminar paper and group discussion.

- As part of fortnightly sessions working with children brought into the college, students were regularly asked to present 'both diagnosis and prognosis' as a result of the activities and assessment they had set up (not for reading only, but for all subjects) (F).

- Keeping a detailed record of what pupils read over a seven- week teaching practice period.

- Again on teaching practice, keeping a record of their pupils' reading, to which parents and children added comments.

Some tutors felt they were paying increasing attention to record- keeping (B; I). This was felt to be a result of the National Curriculum, rather than a consequence of their approach to reading (I).

The description of their approach to record-keeping by the staff on one course (J) may be of interest. Their students, they commented, spent a great deal of time devising records. While on teaching practice, students shared their records of

70

the children's reading with the class teacher. This was felt to change the status of such records and to validate them in the eyes of the teacher. The lecturers also encouraged schools to allow students to become involved in parents' evenings, along with the class teacher, and talk to parents on the basis of the class records that they kept. Interviewees stressed the importance of the students learning from each other's school experience in this respect, by reviewing what had been done in relation to reading on teaching practice; and the sharing of experiences, difficulties or successes.

### 4.7.3   Formal testing

Published reading tests and school and LEA testing policies appeared to be an area to which students were only briefly introduced (A; C; D; I; K). The BEd course on which lecturers insisted that students had to use both a standardised test and a criterion- referenced assessment in the course of their teaching practice 'according to the letter' and 'as written up in the manual' was unusual, as was the course on which students carried out an in-depth study of at least one reading test (C). Generally, the approach of course tutors to formal testing was critical, stressing the limitations of many tests - 'what they do and don't assess' - but only one course admitted to discouraging its students from using traditional tests.

Most courses mentioned coverage of SATs (C; D; I; K; L; O). Local teachers were involved as speakers in some cases; in another, students had worked with Year 2 teachers in schools during the 1991 KS1 SATs period (O).

### 4.7.4   Time constraints on PGCE courses

Not surprisingly, the BEd courses that were discussed in interviews appeared to spend much more time on, or involve their students in more projects relating to, assessment. At one institution where the BEd degree had a strong focus on record-keeping, it was pointed out that PGCE students generally spent two hours considering this topic during their year's course (J).

## 4.8   School experience and teaching practice

### 4.8.1   Issues

Periods of school observation, school visits (serial school experience) and teaching practice are a major aspect of students' training, both in terms of time, and in the influence they have on extending students' knowledge of teaching reading.

Considering courses in detail, there is a lot of variation in the way school experience is structured for students. From the interviews with staff and students, there was no indication of whether any of the many patterns of organisation were more successful than others. Some aspects of the structure and use of school experience were felt to make a difference in increasing its value to students, and increasing the extent to which students' course and school experience were integrated. These were:

- the way in which the courses structured observation periods and set tasks on serial school experience sessions

- the way courses handled the briefing and debriefing of students after short or long sessions of school experience

- the monitoring and assessment of teaching practice, including the informal contacts and advice, and the use of teaching practice files or lesson plans.

The relationship between what students experienced in schools and what they were taught on their courses is a central issue. It raises issues to do with the integration of theoretical and practical knowledge, and with the degree to which students have a chance to experience a variety of methods of teaching reading.

### 4.8.2  School experience

**Definitions and purposes**

The term 'school experience' is here being used to cover all the school or pupil contacts arranged for students apart from their block teaching practices. It includes periods of observation, often placed at the beginning of a course. An important element is 'serial school experience', i.e. students either visit a range of schools, or have regular day or half-day placements in a single school, sometimes in preparation for longer teaching practices in that school. In addition, some institutions bring children into the college either for particular sessions (for example, when covering special needs) or on a regular basis. Sometimes students spend extra time in school collecting data for projects or assignments.

Broadly, such experience is used to extend the students' experience of a range of schools and classrooms and to focus their attention on particular aspects of teaching. Courses often try to make sure that students have a chance to observe or work with children of a range of ages. Observation in primary schools was common on secondary courses; and observation in infant or nursery classrooms in courses for primary students (D; C). Some institutions tried to make sure that students experienced a range of types of schools: for example, urban and rural

(C); monocultural and multicultural (C); 'leafy suburbs' and inner city schools (P).

Schools were sometimes chosen for school experience because they represented good examples of a particular approach to education, e.g. their multicultural policies (H; O). On the whole, however, staff felt that they could not select schools to demonstrate approaches to reading (there were exceptions, which are referred to below). The reasons for this are not completely clear. Courses often prided themselves on their links with schools and teachers in their area, and clearly spent much time negotiating access to schools for students. The problem is perhaps that there are relatively few schools which adopt a single approach to teaching reading. There is also, as one student pointed out, the problem of the potential distance between the school's language policies and what actually goes on in the classroom.

## Observation periods

Some courses placed particular stress on the value of observation. One, for example, emphasised it as one of the competencies they expected students to acquire from the course: to observe children as readers and record their progress as readers (F). There was some variation in the extent to which students were briefed on what to look out for in periods of observation in schools. Teachers were sometimes involved in giving initial briefings and debriefings (M; P). Briefing handbooks for students, often covering not just observation but also other aspects of school practice, were quite common.

## Serial school experience

Courses appear to have more freedom in structuring serial school experience than in influencing teaching practice, in which the students' experience seems to be largely governed by the school context and the classroom teacher.

There appears to be a general movement towards making serial school experience more structured and task-focused. This means that such visits are becoming more closely linked to particular aspects of a student's course or organised to complement lectures and course work (e.g. C; H; L). Only two primary courses seemed to have reservations about introducing more controlled school experience (A; D), and one of these was moving in this direction. One course stressed the difficulties in negotiating such tasks with the school and class teachers (D); but most course tutors were willing to spend a lot of time and effort in just such negotiations (B; H).

Examples of tasks set for students in relation to reading included:

- telling a story to a group or a class
- writing a book or a story for children (often 'Big Books')

- introducing a book or a story to children

- preparing an anthology of books for the classroom

- examining reading schemes used in the classroom

- looking at language and literacy in relation to science and maths (O)

- asking students to assess the language of individual children throughout the year (G).

In most instances the tasks set were supervised by the classroom teacher, written up and reported back in tutor groups. Lecturers on one course stressed data collection for further exploitation as one of the main objectives of serial school experience; this was a course that appeared to have an effective 'action research' ethos (H; also F). Most courses prepared detailed handouts to brief

students on tasks, often including suggestions for obligatory or further reading, and making links to ongoing lectures and course workshops. 'Mini-handbooks' which collected together such tasks and included space for student notes and comments seemed a useful device, in that they allowed lecturers to monitor any student's experiences rapidly (e.g. M).

Sometimes courses managed to control the relationship between the school visit and the associated course work very closely. One example was a morning spent working with bilingual infants, immediately followed by a course session on oral work with bilingual children. Staff on this PGCE course felt that such close links were so important that they blocked the language element of the course for all students at the same point in the course, despite the timetabling difficulties this involved (L).

### 4.8.3 Teaching practice

Teaching practice entails longer periods of placement in schools, ranging from three weeks to a term. Again, there seems to be great diversity in the precise number, timing and length of block teaching practices among courses. The type of school involved and the degree of responsibility given to the student is, as far as possible, vetted or monitored by lecturers, but seldom takes account of the school's language policies.

**Preparation of students for teaching reading on teaching practice**

Block teaching practice at a school was often prepared for by visits to the school (e.g. B; E), sometimes involving a number of serial school experience sessions. Guidelines and checklists were in common use, for example:

- a checklist of aspects to keep in mind during school experience (A)

- guidance for planning for reading (B)

- a handbook covering both serial school experience and block teaching practice
- interviews or tutorials as a preparation (M).

Courses varied in how detailed the teaching plans were that they required of students. The following requirement seems typical of primary courses: the preparation of a language scheme of work including reading, usually referring to NC Attainment Targets and programmes of study, which was discussed both with course tutors and the classroom teacher or school language postholder before implementation.

### Monitoring and evaluation of teaching practice

The kind of records or files that students were required to keep on teaching practice varied, as did the extent to which detailed lessonplans were required. One student commented that, on her course, tutors had their own different requirements, although these were now beginning to be standardised.

Students appeared to be closely monitored by regular visits from tutors. The question of the extent to which such tutors had particular expertise in the teaching of reading was raised. Some primary courses felt that all their staff had expertise in this area (e.g. C; M). Other interviewees saw no alternative to the fact that some students might be supervised by staff with subject interests other than English (and were sometimes at pains to point out that despite the importance of reading, there were other aspects of teaching for which they had the responsibility to prepare students). In other courses, it was implied that this supervision by non-specialist staff, though inevitable, was a weakness on their courses (A; I). One interviewee had recently circulated guidelines to colleagues, but was not sanguine as to their effect. In two courses, there appeared to be tutor follow-through from the language part of the course to teaching practice (L; O).

While there were wide variations as to which of the teaching practices that students undertook counted towards year or degree assessments, all teaching practices appeared to be monitored and evaluated. Staff on one course referred to involving teachers in developing their criteria for assessment (K). Students were sometimes involved in their own evaluation (C; J; K) and appreciated this (K student); others were not initially aware of the criteria against which they were being assessed (A). Some examples of ways in which students were involved in evaluating their own performance in teaching reading were:

- All forms used by tutors had space for student comments.
- In Year 3 of one BEd course, a Record of Achievement was used to help students reflect on reading work, and to set themselves targets (J).
- Year 3 students drew up a c.v. to be sent to their preferred teaching practice school; the last section of this stated what they felt they needed to address during teaching practice. At the end of the practice they again stated the areas needing attention (K).

The monitoring or evaluation schedules used to evaluate or assess student performance on teaching practice varied. Commonly, these did not refer specifically to reading, although sometimes 'English' was specified; more often, the area was covered under a general heading, such as 'Professional Applications' (D). However, most lecturers interviewed were confident that students who were having difficulties in teaching reading would be 'picked up' (D; J). Some interviewees felt that the level of generality of assessment documentation was inevitable: it was not under their control but had to be negotiated with colleagues; more detailed schedules would be unworkable (B). Some changes were in hand, though not necessarily related to reading. One form was being revised to pay more attention to group work (B); another institution was experimenting with a competence-based approach to assessment.

The debriefing of students after teaching practice was generally felt to be important too (e.g. B; F; J), for example a seminar designed specifically to look at the teaching of reading to 'unpack' what students had learned (F; J). Some courses placed much emphasis on students sharing their school experiences with one another, in debriefing sessions or workshops, or in the form of seminar papers and the like. They felt that it was important that students learn from each others' experience. Tutors on one primary BEd course had been experimenting with bringing Year 4 students together with first-year students, and reported that this had been very successful. Encouraging students to reflect on their experiences was sometimes handled in other ways. For example, a tutor of an upper primary BEd course, in which Year 1 students had developed and used a plan of work during their teaching practice, later asked the students to produce a written evaluation of their plan and its success.

The assumption that the course-based parts of teacher training essentially cover theoretical issues, whereas school experience accounts for practice is a questionable one. Courses are, in the main, not highly theoretical; and as one interviewee pointed out, students confront theoretical issues in school and are confronted with practical issues within college-based courses. It should be said that helping students to gain maximum benefit from all aspects of their course and ensuring the coherence of the course as a whole require much care in planning, organisation and school liaison. This is an aspect of course preparation and development that it is sometimes difficult to gauge in the course of an interview.

### 4.8.4   *Integration of coursework and school experience*

Interviews with students were revealing about the extent to which there were mismatches between what they were taught on their courses, and what they encountered in schools. Generally, this became an issue only when courses had, or were perceived as having, a particular bias. Otherwise, students were more likely to complain that they had not seen a sufficient range of approaches in action. A disparity in resources between schools and courses, or at least the unavailability in schools of what students had been told was desirable, was remarked on as often as were differences in approach. Not all students felt that there was a mismatch between what they were taught in their course and what they encountered on teaching practice. Some did. Sometimes they felt this was inevitable: they were very clear that on teaching practice they had to 'fit in' - the phrase occurred several times. The students interviewed had independent views: criticism of college/course practice and of school practice was distributed in roughly equal measure. There were comments, for example, to the effect that:

- it would have been nice to be taken to more schools where policies do match what children are taught

- it would have been nice to encounter more schools where phonics were used, and worked

- it was always interesting to see 'bad schemes' in action, particularly 'when what the college said was "bad" worked'.

Some of the examples of 'mismatch' identified by students who were interviewed follow. There are comments on differences in the approaches recommended by courses and found in schools, but equally frequently students appeared to be unhappy that they had not had the chance to try out particular approaches. In other cases, the problems they had encountered centred on practical constraints or lack of resources in schools.

The examples given were:

- Bilingual books were not available in a school. Taking some in smacked of 'tokenism'.

- The course's emphasis on holding writers' workshops and reading conferences did not tally with the time available in schools.

- The demands of the NC were felt more sharply in schools.

- Finding teachers with 'different' approaches to children's spellings was difficult.

- The 'push to real books' did not match the emphasis on reading schemes in school.

- Some students found an emphasis on phonics in infant schools which was not reflected in college work.

- The college always talked about the 'ideal' situation - but 'what if you don't get a collaborative teacher, you don't get good reading schemes - you may find a poor reading corner'.

- There was an instance where 'college learning only came in' when the student concerned was allowed to develop a book corner.

Students encountered challenges in schools that they did not feel they had been prepared for, although these kinds of problems are perhaps inevitable if students are to be involved in teaching practice throughout their courses. For example, a student on a Year 2 teaching practice was faced with a boy who couldn't read. She commented that, as she hadn't touched on this possibility in her course, all she could do was use her intuition. Another student complained that in her course there had been nothing said about relationships with the class teacher or with parents.

Other students wanted more thorough preparation in certain areas. For example, one individual wanted to know 'how to use schemes effectively, because all the schools use them' (in her course, she had looked at *Ginn*, *Gay Way*, *Story Chest* and *Oxford Reading Tree*, but felt this was not sufficient preparation for actually using any of these schemes). Several students wanted more preparation that involved practical applications, strategies and resources for children with particular needs. In one interview, a number of students felt that their course offered 'information not practicalities' ('you couldn't go into a school and use it').

If courses are really being eclectic rather than prescriptive in the methods of teaching reading that they recommend, a degree of 'mismatch' in approaches taken by college and school is not necessarily disadvantageous, as long as students accept that a variety of different ways of teaching reading can be effective, and provided that they encounter a range of approaches across their school experience. Students commented on the value of experiencing different approaches at first hand. One, for example, explained that in her first school, she felt the teacher was using an inappropriate test and 'a very bad scheme'; she commented that the children were not enjoying it. In her last school, teachers were using flashcards and group and shared reading, and 'it worked well'. Other students commented that they had not experienced a wide enough range of practice; one student complained that she had only been in schools that used '*Ginn* and real books'. Obviously, this lack of exposure to a range of methods is a particular problem on PGCE courses, given the limited time at their disposal.

## 4.9   The future  of teacher training

In interviews in relation to at least one primary BEd and one secondary PGCE course, the uncertainty affecting future teacher training courses in England and Wales was said to be deleterious.  One interviewee suggested that it hardly mattered if minor changes were made to CATE criteria in relation to reading, given that the entire future of his institution was in doubt.

Other lecturers expressed the concern that teacher training that was predominantly school-based could not allow students access to sufficient experience of a variety of methods of teaching reading. Nor, it was suggested, could the - admittedly limited - theoretical elements of the current training courses be dismissed.  Teachers are immersed in practice in their everyday jobs; the challenge for training courses was to link practical and theoretical concerns. In one case, the 'virtuous circle' between theory and practice and theory and research was stressed.

The balance between main subject study and professional applications came in for some criticism.  One interviewee commented that it was currently 1:1.  He would have liked to see a shift to 1:2 or 1:3 in favour of teaching applications.

# The Graduate Questionnaire

**by Tom Gorman**

# THE GRADUATE QUESTIONNAIRE

## 5.1 The approach

It was thought necessary to obtain some evidence from the graduates of a number of the courses about which detailed information had been obtained.

Accordingly, a questionnaire for graduates was developed (this is reproduced in Appendix D to this volume), and the 20 institutions that had been selected to participate in the programme of visits and staff interviews were asked to forward the questionnaire to all the 1991 graduates of one specified course at each institution. Six institutions declined to do so; the main reasons given for non-involvement were the non-availability or inaccessibility of student records at the time in question. Fourteen institutions agreed to forward questionnaires to students or to provide the NFER with information for this purpose. Replies were received from 413 graduates from 13 of these institutions. Approximately one in three of the graduates to whom questionnaires were forwarded returned them by the deadline suggested.

There were widely differing rates of response from graduates of the different institutions. Over half of the questionnaires returned came from graduates of four institutions. In contrast, only four graduates replied from another institution.

The sample of responses received was not therefore a random sample and this should be taken account of in the interpretation of the findings. The great majority of teachers in the sample were **new teachers,** that is, **they had been in post for at most one month**. This fact must be borne in mind when interpreting data from the graduate questionnaire. No information was sought from experienced teachers, since this was not a specification for this project.

## 5.2 The sample

Of the 413 respondents, 344 (83 per cent) had found teaching posts, of whom approximately two-thirds were in primary schools. The remainder were teachers in secondary schools or other institutions. Figure 5.2.1 illustrates this distribution.

*Figure 5.2.1  Current teaching of respondents*

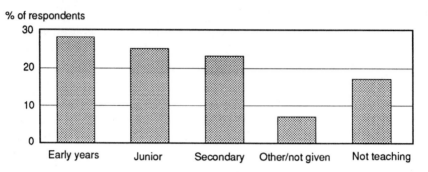

Figure 5.2.2 shows the percentages of graduates who were or were not teaching pupils of the age-range for which they had been trained.

*Figure 5.2.2   Age-range of training and age-range of teaching*

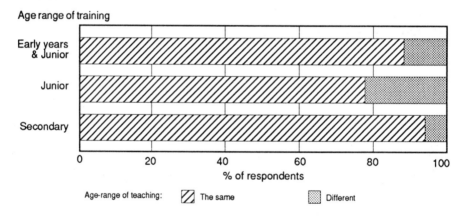

Because not all the institutions which were asked to participate in the graduate survey were able to do so, this sample contained **no** teachers who had been trained to teach only early years, that is, no graduates from courses which had focused exclusively on ages four to eight. Overall, almost 90 per cent of those in the sample who were in teaching posts were teaching pupils of the age-range for which they had been trained.

Forty-four per cent of the graduates had taken BEd courses, and 56 per cent PGCE courses. Figure 5.2.3 illustrates the distribution of BEd and PGCE graduates overall and by age-range of course. Just over half of the PGCE graduates in the sample (52 per cent) were teaching pupils in primary schools and about half of these were responsible for pupils in the early years.

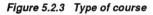
Figure 5.2.3 Type of course

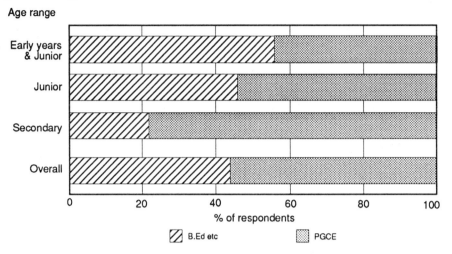

Not all graduates in the sample who were currently in teaching posts were responsible for teaching reading, but most (74 per cent) did have this responsibility. Virtually all teachers in primary schools (95 per cent), but only a quarter (26 per cent) of those in secondary schools considered themselves to be responsible for the teaching of reading.

## 5.3    The theory and practice of reading

### 5.3.1  General

The graduates were asked the following question:

AT THE END OF THE YOUR COURSE, HOW CONFIDENT DID YOU FEEL ABOUT THE FOLLOWING AREAS?

1.     Knowledge about language

2.     Knowledge about the process of reading

3.     Knowledge about methods of teaching reading

4.     Practice in the application of this knowledge in the classroom.

It was thought important to make distinctions between a) knowledge that was primarily theoretical in nature about aspects of language and the process of reading; b) knowledge about the methodology of teaching reading; c) practice in the application of these areas of knowledge in the classroom.

No value judgements are implied here. We broadly subscribe to the view that a theoretical grounding in the disciplines relevant to the teaching of reading is part of a good foundation for good practice. It is not, of course, a substitute for it.

Figure 5.3.1 illustrates the general pattern of response to the four questions.

**Figure 5.3.1  Confidence at the  end of the course**

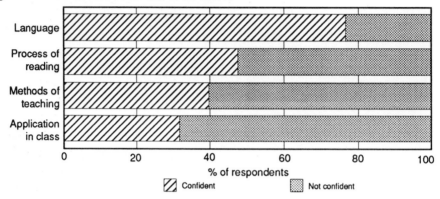

Figure 5.3.2 presents the same information in relation to the age-range of the courses taken by the graduates.

**Figure 5.3.2  Confidence at the end of the course by age-range of course**

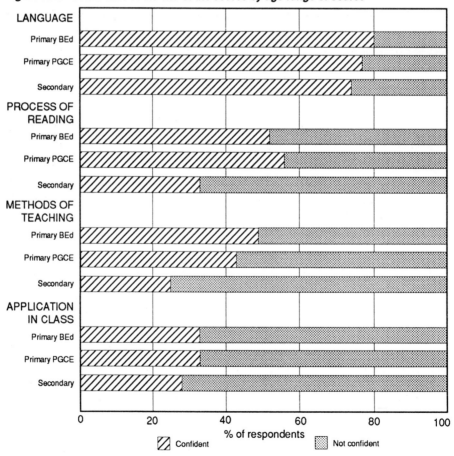

### 5.3.2 Knowledge about language

Whatever the age-range for which they had been prepared to teach, between 70 and 80 per cent of the graduates felt confident about their 'knowledge about language'. This area of study was the central concern of the Working Party that produced the Kingman Report (DES, 1988a), which the majority of students would have had access to. Some of the main elements of the report are, in turn, incorporated into the knowledge about language (KAL) strands of the National Curriculum attainment targets in English.

It needs to be said, however, that the National Curriculum does not require that teachers should have a knowledge of the main features of the sound system (or phonology) of English. Neither does it require that teachers should have a knowledge of the complex ways in which those elements of the sound system that distinguish vowels and diphthongs, for example, relate to the orthography of English. This information is of particular relevance to the diagnosis of systematic errors that pupils may make in reading aloud, for example. Such knowledge is also necessary for an intelligent interpretation of different approaches to the teaching of phonics and the claims made with respect to these.

It is clear, however, from the review of the reading assignments associated with the courses taken and from interviews with teaching staff that the **systematic** study of language is not a significant component of the majority of the courses taken by the graduates. The basis for the high degree of confidence shown with respect to 'knowledge about language' may therefore be questioned.

### 5.3.3 Knowledge about the process of reading

Just over half of the sample as a whole lacked confidence with respect to this area of knowledge. A distinction was, however, apparent between graduates trained for work in primary schools and those destined for careers at secondary level. Over half of the former were confident about their knowledge of the process of reading, whereas only a third of the graduates prepared for work in secondary schools demonstrated such confidence.

### 5.3.4 Knowledge about methods of teaching reading

In the sample as a whole, 40 per cent of the teachers said that they felt very confident or fairly confident with respect to their knowledge about methods of teaching reading.

Teachers trained to teach at secondary level were, again, more likely to lack confidence in their knowledge about such methods than were teachers trained to teach at primary level. Three-quarters of the secondary group expressed a lack of confidence in this aspect of professional work, whereas about six out of ten teachers trained to teach at junior level (62 per cent) and four out of ten (44 per cent) of the graduates trained for work with pupils in the early and junior years were confident about their knowledge of such methods.

The fact that over half of the teachers trained to teach at primary level lacked such confidence reflects a state of affairs that is not substantially different from the situation that obtained when the HMI survey of New Teachers in Schools was undertaken in 1987 (DES, 1988b).


## 5.3.5 Classroom application of the knowledge gained

Just over 30 per cent of the graduates said that they felt confident at the end of their course with regard to practice in the application of the knowledge they had gained in the classroom. It is understandable that, at the end of a period of initial teaching training and on first entry to school, only three out of ten teachers should feel confident about applying the theoretical, technical and methodological information gained in college in a classroom context. From another perspective, however, their relative lack of confidence raises questions to do with the the nature of the integration of course work and school experience. This issue is dealt with in a specific section of the questionnaire.

Teachers trained for work with pupils in the primary years were no more confident about the classroom applications of what they knew (33 per cent) than were teachers who had prepared for work in secondary schools (28 per cent).

The responses of students who had taken different types of courses were not dissimilar. BEd students were just as likely to have confidence or to lack it in matters to do with knowledge about language, knowledge about the process of reading and classroom applications of such knowledge as were students who took PGCE courses. Only in regard to their knowledge about methods of teaching reading was there a moderate difference between the two groups. Forty six per cent of the graduates with BEds, as opposed to 36 per cent of those with GCEs, expressed confidence in their acquaintance with methods of teaching reading at the end of their course.

## 5.4 Approaches to the teaching of reading

### 5.4.1 General

The graduates were also asked an open-ended question about the approaches to reading that they were taught about.

The question was:

> WHAT APPROACHES TO READING WERE YOU TAUGHT ABOUT IN YOUR RECENT COURSE?

There were no substantive differences between the nature of the answers given by students in one-year or four-year courses in most respects.

The main approaches mentioned (in caption form) and the proportions referring to them are given in Figure 5.4.1.

Figure 5.4.1 Approaches to reading taught about

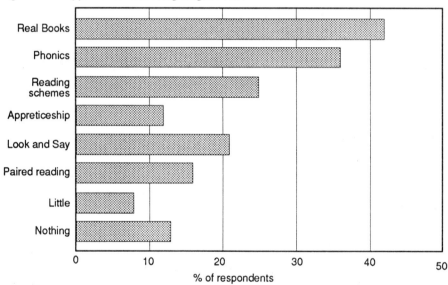

No other method or approach (e.g. language experience, miscue analysis or approaches entailing parental involvement) was referred to by more than five per cent of the graduates. The question therefore served to differentiate the most common approaches presented in training courses at this particular time.

As one would expect, there were substantial differences between the types of answers given by teachers trained to teach at secondary level and their colleagues trained at primary level. Nearly half (47 per cent) of the former, as opposed to 12 per cent of the latter, claimed to have been taught little or nothing about approaches to the teaching of reading.

### 5.4.2 Phonics

The teaching of phonics and the place of phonics in the teaching of initial literacy is a topic on which there has been a considerable amount of discussion in recent months. For this reason, the graduates were asked, in an open-ended question, to give more information about what they were taught in their course about phonic approaches to reading.

The question was:

WHAT WERE YOU TAUGHT IN YOUR COURSE ABOUT PHONIC APPROACHES TO READING?

Three hundred and eighty-seven graduates responded, of whom approximately six out of ten (60 per cent) said that they had been taught little or nothing about phonics. Nineteen per cent said that they had been taught about the teaching of phonics in combination with other methods.

Over 80 per cent of the graduates trained to work at secondary level and over half (52 per cent) of the teachers prepared for work in primary school claimed to have had little or no teaching about phonics.

### 5.4.3 Other aspects of the teaching of reading

A further question referred to specific aspects of reading covered in some courses. The graduates were asked, firstly, to say if a particular aspect of reading was covered in the course they had taken and, secondly, to say how confident they felt about this aspect of reading.

The responses indicate that the aspects listed had been covered in 43-84 per cent of the courses given.

The aspects referred to, and the degree of confidence felt by graduates in the applicability of what they knew about them, are shown in Figure 5.4.2. Figure 5. 4.3 provides a primary/secondary breakdown of this information. Graduates who, in their own view, had not been taught about the aspects of reading in question, understandably tended to lack confidence in their ability to use these aspects in teaching.

**Figure 5.4.2** *Confidence at the end of the course in nine aspects of the teaching of reading, by coverage*

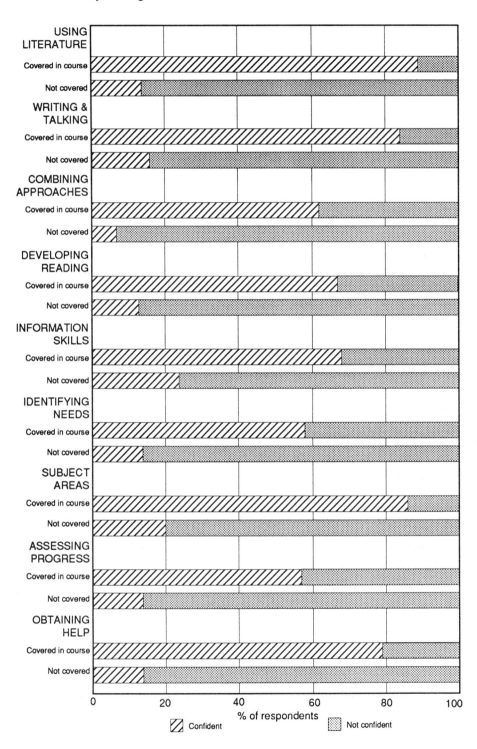

**Figure 5.4.3   Confidence at the end of the course in nine aspects of the teaching of reading, by age-range of course**

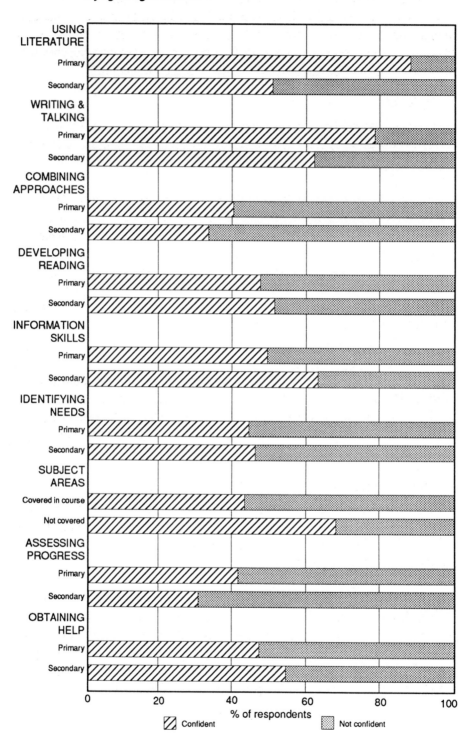

USING LITERATURE
Primary
Secondary

WRITING & TALKING
Primary
Secondary

COMBINING APPROACHES
Primary
Secondary

DEVELOPING READING
Primary
Secondary

INFORMATION SKILLS
Primary
Secondary

IDENTIFYING NEEDS
Primary
Secondary

SUBJECT AREAS
Covered in course
Not covered

ASSESSING PROGRESS
Primary
Secondary

OBTAINING HELP
Primary
Secondary

0    20    40    60    80    100
% of respondents

Confident          Not confident

### Using literature

Most teachers trained for primary schools and over half of those trained to teach in secondary schools had studied issues relating to the use of children's literature in their training courses. Correspondingly, most teachers at primary level (88 per cent) and just over half (54 per cent) of the secondary teachers felt confident about their knowledge of this aspect of the teaching of reading.

### Links with writing and talking

Over 80 per cent of the graduates said that they had been exposed to teaching about links with talking and writing during their courses of initial training, and most (74 per cent) had confidence in what they knew.

### Selecting, sequencing and combining approaches to the teaching of reading

Two-thirds of the teachers trained to work with pupils in the primary years said that issues relating to selecting and combining approaches to the teaching of reading had been covered in the course they had taken, and four out of ten (40 per cent) felt confident about what they had learnt. A third (32 per cent) of the graduates who had been prepared to work at secondary level said that the topic was covered in the courses taken, and a similar proportion (34 per cent) felt confidence in the applicability of what they had learnt.

### Developing and extending reading

Approximately half of the graduates in the sample were confident about this area of the teaching of reading. There was little difference in this respect between teachers trained to work at different stages, although this aspect is generally, and perhaps erroneously, thought to be more relevant to the teaching of reading after the initial stages.

### Information and study skills

With regard to the teaching of study skills that would need to be applied in reading for learning, teachers trained to teach at secondary level tended to be more confident in what they knew (63 per cent) than those trained for work with pupils at primary level (49 per cent).

### Identifying pupils with special educational needs (including dyslexia)

Two-thirds of the graduates reported that the topic of dyslexia was dealt with in their courses. Forty-five per cent of the sample felt a degree of confidence in the applicability of what they knew, there being very little variation in this respect between teachers concerned with primary or secondary level. Conversely, more than half of those responding (55 per cent) lacked confidence in this area.

### Reading in specific subject areas

According to the graduates, some attention had been given to the reading demands of specific subject areas, in two thirds of the courses given for secondary teachers (65 per cent), and in one third of the courses given for teachers of pupils at primary level (35 per cent). Approximately four out of ten teachers of primary pupils (43 per cent), and seven out of ten graduates trained to teach in secondary schools (68 per cent), were confident that they knew sufficient about the area to make use of their knowledge in teaching.

### Assessing reading progress

Sixty-six per cent of the teachers trained to teach at primary level said that they had received instruction in issues to do with the assessment of reading whereas less than a third of the secondary graduates had done so, according to their responses. Despite this, the difference in the proportions of graduates concerned with primary and secondary pupils who had confidence in ability to apply such knowledge was not great. Just over 40 per cent of those who had taken primary courses and 30 per cent of those trained for secondary level felt confident about assessing progress in reading.

### Knowing where to obtain help

According to their answers, over half of the graduates had been given information in their courses about where to obtain help on matters to do with teaching reading; and almost a half were confident about being able to make use of this information.

## 5.5   The integration of coursework and school experience

Students were asked about the integration of coursework (lectures, seminars, essays, private study, etc.) with their school experience in particular relation to:

(a)   methods of teaching reading

(b)   materials used

(c)   the assessment of reading.

The question was:

> IN YOUR OPINION, WAS YOUR COURSEWORK (LECTURES, SEMINARS, ESSAYS, PRIVATE STUDY, ETC.) WELL INTEGRATED WITH YOUR SCHOOL EXPERIENCE IN RELATION TO THE FOLLOWING AREAS?

The pattern of responses given by graduates who had taken different types of courses is given in Figure 5.5.1.

**Figure 5.5.1 Integration of course work and school experience**

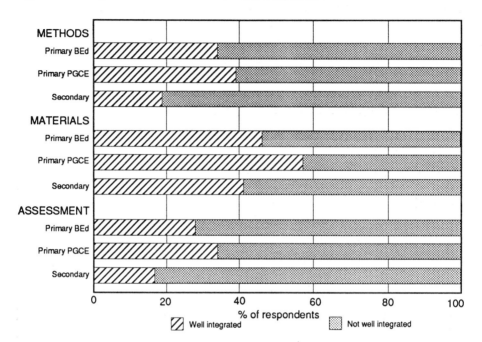

### Methods of teaching reading

In the sample as a whole, three out of ten graduates (32 per cent) felt that their course work had been well integrated with their school experience in terms of methods of teaching reading. Only two out of ten graduates of courses aimed at secondary level felt this to be the case, however, as compared to nearly four out of ten teachers who trained to work in primary school.

### Materials used

Just under half of the graduates responding (48 per cent) thought that there had been effective integration as regards the materials used in their course work and their school experience.

### The assessment of reading

A rather lower proportion of graduates (27 per cent) thought that course work and school experience had been well integrated with respect to the assessment of reading. Again, teachers with primary training were more likely than teachers trained for secondary level to report this (31 per cent of the former as opposed to 17 per cent of the latter).

## 5.6 Aspects in which more help was required

In a concluding question, the graduates were asked: 'Are there any other aspects of teaching reading in regard to which you would have liked to have more help during your course?' The ten most frequent responses are listed in Figure 5.6.1.

**Figure 5.6.1 Issues on which graduates would have liked more help**

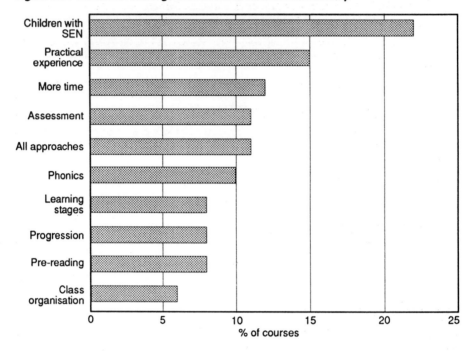

The area of need mentioned by the largest group of graduates (22 per cent) concerned the assessment of children with special educational needs.

Fifteen per cent of the graduates indicated that they would have benefited from having more practical experience of teaching reading, and 11 per cent wanted more time generally devoted to this area.

Twelve per cent of those trained to teach at primary level felt the need for more information about phonics.

Over a third (36 per cent) of the graduates trained to teach secondary pupils indicated that they did not think that a concern with the teaching of reading was directly relevant to teaching at secondary level. Several mentioned that those in secondary teaching made the assumption, rightly or wrongly, that children would be able to read competently when they reached secondary school. Several also saw the teaching of reading as being relevant only to teachers dealing with special needs.

# REFERENCES

KINGMAN REPORT. GREAT BRITAIN. DEPARTMENT OF EDUCATION AND SCIENCE (1988a). *Report of the Committee of Inquiry into the Teaching of English Language London: HMSO.*

GREAT BRITAIN. DEPARTMENT OF EDUCATION AND SCIENCE (1988b) *New Teachers in Schools: a Survey by HMI.* London: HMSO.

# APPENDICES

## Appendix A: The Project Staff

Dr. Tom Gorman, Principal Research Officer and Project Director

Dr. Greg Brooks, Senior Research Officer and Project Leader

Ms. Lesley Kendall, Senior Research Officer and Project Statistician

Ms. Alison Tate, Senior Research Officer

Ms. Effie de Souza, Project Secretary

In addition, some fieldwork interviews were conducted by

Ms. Janet White and Ms. Anne Kispal of the Centre for Research in Language and Communication at the NFER,

and by

Mr. John Harman, consultant.

# Appendix B: List of Members and Assessors of the CATE Working Group

| | |
|---|---|
| Professor Sir William Taylor | Chairperson, CATE |
| Professor Robin Alexander | Professor of Primary Education<br>University of Leeds |
| Mr. John Burn | Headmaster<br>Longbenton Community High School |
| Professor Brian Cox | Pro-Vice Chancellor<br>University of Manchester |
| Mr. Pratap Deshpande | Policy Adviser,<br>Development and Review<br>Birmingham Education Department |
| Mrs. Gay Firth | Journalist, Financial Times |
| Professor Elizabeth Goodacre | Middlesex Polytechnic |
| Dr. Seamus Hegarty | Deputy Director<br>National Foundation for Educational<br>Research |
| Mr. Anthony Lenney | Chief Education Officer Wakefield |
| Mrs. Margaret Pritchard | Headteacher, Wat's Dyke Infant<br>School, North Wales |

## Assessors

| | |
|---|---|
| SI Mr. Michael Convey | Her Majesty's Inspectorate |
| Mr. John Whitaker | Department of Education and Science |
| Mr. Chris Woodhead/<br>Ms. Alix Beleschenko | National Curriculum Council |

## Secretariat

| | |
|---|---|
| Dr. Edward Schuldt (Secretary) | CATE Secretariat |
| Mr. David Hook | CATE Secretariat |

# Appendix C: The Institutional Questionnaire

N.B. This questionnaire was originally A4 and has been photo reduced for reproduction in this volume.

 **Council for the Accreditation of Teacher Education**

# Questionnaire
# on Initial Teacher Training
# for the Teaching of Reading

Institution:..................................................................................................................................

Contact:......................................................................................................................................

## Aims and Objectives

The aim of this survey is to gather information about how students are prepared to teach reading in primary and secondary schools. It is being undertaken by the National Foundation for Educational Research on behalf of the Council for the Accreditation of Teacher Education (CATE) which has been asked by the Secretary of State to report on training for the teaching of reading.

We realise that completion of this questionnaire will take up time and attention at a busy period in the academic year. It is essential, however, that the fullest possible information about how teachers are prepared to teach reading is available to CATE, and your help in providing that information will be very much appreciated. Provision of existing documentation will be welcome (see page 2).

## Code of Practice

The answers you provide to the questionnaire will be treated in strict confidence. No individual, course or institution will be identified in NFER's report to CATE, or in any report or publication arising from the research.

## Information for contact person

You have been sent a number of questionnaires. We would be grateful if you would ensure that one questionnaire is completed for each ITT course (primary and secondary) run by the institution in which **explicit attention is given to preparing students to teach reading**.

If you pass questionnaires on to course leaders or other individuals for completion, please (1) respect the confidentiality of their replies when they pass through your hands; (2) take responsibility for checking that the questionnaires are completed and returned to us BY 1ST JULY 1991 at the following address: CATE Enquiry
National Foundation for Educational Research
The Mere
Upton Park
Slough SL1 2DQ

If you have any queries, please contact either Greg Brooks or Alison Tate at NFER, Tel: (0753) 74123 (till 17 June) (0753) 574123 (from 18 June).

---

### THANK YOU FOR YOUR HELP.

## Information for respondent

a)   Except for question 16, the questions in this questionnaire ask you for information only on the training in the teaching of reading that ALL students on the course are exposed to, i.e. the MINIMUM or CORE or COMPULSORY coverage of reading in the course.

b)   If it is difficult to determine which elements of the course constitute the CORE (e.g. if the course is modular), please answer in terms of the most typical route through the course.

c)   Please DO NOT include in the definition of the CORE any coverage of reading which forms part of the training of only some students on the course, e.g.
   -   English specialisms
   -   optional courses on or including reading.

d)   In addition to completing and returning the questionnaire, we would be most grateful if you would attach to it documents relevant to:
   i)    the preparation of students for the teaching of reading in the core or compulsory elements of the course
   ii)   the preparation of students for the teaching of reading in English as a specialist subject
   iii)  any reading element in other subject specialisms
   iv)   any optional courses on or including reading.

   Where possible, please ensure that this material includes:

   -   information about school experience elements of the course
   -   course timetables and structure diagrams if available
   -   reading lists (if possible distinguish between compulsory and recommended reading).

   You may wish to refer to this material in some of your responses. If so, please make sure the reference is specific and the documents referred to are attached to the questionnaire.

e)   The questions in the questionnaire either ask you to provide specific information or invite more extended responses. For some questions, space is given for answer by year of course, up to year 4. If you are responding for a shorter course please fill in only the relevant years (e.g. Year 1 in the case of a one year PGCE).

f)   When you have completed the questionnaire, please
   -   attach to it any relevant documents
   -   place the questionnaire and documents in a sealed envelope
   -   write on the envelope the title of the course to which the completed questionnaire refers
   -   return the envelope to the person named on the front cover, who has been asked to return it to **NFER BY 1ST JULY 1991**.

# Background Information

1. Title of course

   .........................................................................................................................

2. Part-time course/ full- time course  (Circle whichever applies)
3. Length of course       ............... years
4. Honours course?       YES/NO   (Circle whichever applies)
5. Qualification aimed at:                                      **(Tick any which apply)**
       BEd
       BA + Cert. Ed.
       BSc + Cert. Ed.
       PGCE
       Other (please specify)   ...................

6. Age range of pupils that students are being prepared to teach:

                           ...........yrs.  to ...........yrs.

## Training for the teaching of reading in the CORE or COMPULSORY elements of the course

| Staff involved | teaching full-time on THIS course | teaching part-time on THIS course |
|---|---|---|
| 7a) On the core/compulsory elements of the course, how many staff are involved in preparing students to teach reading? | | |
| b) Please indicate how many of these staff have: | | |
| i) Recent (i.e. within the last two years) experience of teaching reading in early years | | |
| ii) Other recent experience of teaching reading in schools | | |
| iii) Experience of teaching pupils with learning difficulties | | |
| iv) Postgraduate qualifications in: | | |
| Linguistics or applied linguistics | | |
| Psychology | | |
| Other relevant subjects (e.g. Language in Education) | | |

Please state which ......................................

18-21

22-25

26-29

30-33

34-37

38-41

42-45

46-47

3

# Time allocated to the teaching of reading

**8. Please indicate, for each year of the course:**

a) How many hours of staff-student contact time are allocated to the area of language (including reading):

48–49

| | | | |
|---|---|---|---|
| Year 1 | ...... hours | Year 3 | ...... hours |
| Year 2 | ...... hours | Year 4 | ...... hours |

50–51<br>52–53<br>54–55

b) Within this total, how many hours of staff-student contact time are allocated specifically to reading?

| | | | |
|---|---|---|---|
| Year 1 | ...... hours | Year 3 | ...... hours |
| Year 2 | ...... hours | Year 4 | ...... hours |

56–57<br>58–59<br>60–61<br>62–63

## Approaches to early reading

**9a) Please look at the following list of approaches to the teaching of early reading, and for each, indicate how much attention it is given in the course (if none, please enter zero):**

CAR

| | Year(s) of course (Circle all that apply) | Hours of staff-student contact time involved across all years of course | Estimate of student non-contact hours involved across all years | Teaching/delivery mode (tick all that apply) | | | | |
|---|---|---|---|---|---|---|---|---|
| | | | | Lectures/ Seminars | Essays | Guided reading | Practical or school-based projects | Focus in teaching practice |
| A Phonic approach | 1 2 3 4 | | | | | | | |
| A 'Look and Say' approach | 1 2 3 4 | | | | | | | |
| A 'Language Experience' approach | 1 2 3 4 | | | | | | | |
| A 'Real Books' approach | 1 2 3 4 | | | | | | | |
| Use of available clues (e.g. context, pictures) to decipher new words | 1 2 3 4 | | | | | | | |
| An integrated approach to reading and writing | 1 2 3 4 | | | | | | | |
| Schemes involving parents at home | 1 2 3 4 | | | | | | | |
| Selection of fiction and non-fiction materials for early readers | 1 2 3 4 | | | | | | | |
| Selection of reading schemes | 1 2 3 4 | | | | | | | |
| What other approaches or issues are covered? ................................ | 1 2 3 4 | | | | | | | |
| ................................ | 1 2 3 4 | | | | | | | |
| ................................ | 1 2 3 4 | | | | | | | |

6<br>19<br>32<br>45<br>58<br>CAR<br>6<br>19<br>32<br>45<br>58<br>60<br>CAR<br>6<br>8<br>21<br>23

Which reading schemes, if any, are recommended?

36-37
38-39
40-41
42-43
44-45
46-47
48-49
50-51

...............................................................................................................

...............................................................................................................

...............................................................................................................

b) Please comment in as much detail as you wish on what students are taught on the course about selecting, sequencing or combining different approaches to the teaching of reading:

52-53
54-55
56-57
58-59
60-61

...............................................................................................................

...............................................................................................................

...............................................................................................................

...............................................................................................................

...............................................................................................................

...............................................................................................................

...............................................................................................................

## Developing reading

10. Please explain what attention is given in the course to ways of developing and extending pupils' reading.

62-63
64-65
66-67
68-69
70-71

...............................................................................................................

...............................................................................................................

...............................................................................................................

...............................................................................................................

...............................................................................................................

...............................................................................................................

...............................................................................................................

# Assessment

**11a)** Please look at the following list of topics related to the assessment of reading, and for each, indicate how much attention it is given in the course (if none, please enter zero):

| | Year(s) of course (Circle all that apply) | Hours of staff-student contact time involved across all years of course | Estimate of student non-contact hours involved across all years | Teaching/delivery mode (tick all that apply) | | | | | CARD |
|---|---|---|---|---|---|---|---|---|---|
| | | | | Lectures/ Seminars | Essays | Guided reading | Practical or school-based projects | Focus in teaching practice | |
| Using a variety of informal assessment methods (e.g. miscue analysis) | 1 2 3 4 | | | | | | | | 6–18 |
| Using published reading tests (diagnostic and/or standardised) | 1 2 3 4 | | | | | | | | 19–31 |
| Methods of assessment of National Curriculum Statements of Attainment (Teacher Assessment) | 1 2 3 4 | | | | | | | | 32–44 |
| Methods of assessment of National Curriculum Statements of Attainment (SATs) | 1 2 3 4 | | | | | | | | 45–57 |
| Keeping records and monitoring progression | 1 2 3 4 | | | | | | | | 58–70 |
| Other (please write in main topics) ............................ | 1 2 3 4 | | | | | | | | CARD 6–7 8–20 |
| ............................ | 1 2 3 4 | | | | | | | | 21–22 23–35 |
| ............................ | 1 2 3 4 | | | | | | | | 36–37 38–50 |
| ............................ | 1 2 3 4 | | | | | | | | 51–52 53–65 |

**b)** Please explain in what ways the course ensures that students develop the capacity to identify gifted pupils and pupils with special educational needs (e.g. dyslexia), and to plan and organise ways in which the potential of such pupils can be developed.

6–7
8–9
10–11
12–13
14–15

..................................................................................................................

..................................................................................................................

..................................................................................................................

## Applied aspects of course

12. **Please explain what planned opportunities exist for students to practise the teaching of reading (i.e. how are the taught courses carried through into students' school experience?):**

16–17
18–19
20–21
22–23
24–25

.......................................................................................................................

.......................................................................................................................

.......................................................................................................................

.......................................................................................................................

.......................................................................................................................

.................;.................................................................................................

## Changes in the course

13. **In what ways, specifically, have the reading elements of the course changed in response to the introduction of the National Curriculum?**

26–27
28–29
30–31
32–33
34–35
36–37

.......................................................................................................................

.......................................................................................................................

.......................................................................................................................

.......................................................................................................................

.......................................................................................................................

.......................................................................................................................

14. **What changes, if any, are planned for the reading elements of the course in the next two years?**

38–39
40–41
42–43
44–45
46–47

.......................................................................................................................

.......................................................................................................................

.......................................................................................................................

.......................................................................................................................

.......................................................................................................................

.......................................................................................................................

15. **If the CATE criteria were to be altered to require explicit courses in the teaching of reading for all students in ITT, what, in your view, would be the implications of this for:**

a) that part of the course concerned with language/English?

b) other parts of the course?

48–49
50–51
52–53
54–55
56–57
58–59

...................................................................................................................................

...................................................................................................................................

...................................................................................................................................

...................................................................................................................................

...................................................................................................................................

## Subject specialisms and reading options

16. Please provide here a list of the documents (asked for in note d on page 2) which you are returning with the questionnaire.

   **Please also indicate on what pages in each document we will find information on reading elements in English specialisms, other subject specialisms and optional parts of the course.**

60–61
62–63
64–65
66–67

...................................................................................................................................

...................................................................................................................................

...................................................................................................................................

...................................................................................................................................

...................................................................................................................................

17. **Please use this space for further comments on any issues raised in the questionnaire, if you wish.**

68–69
70–71
72–73
74–75

...................................................................................................................................

...................................................................................................................................

...................................................................................................................................

...................................................................................................................................

---

**THANK YOU VERY MUCH FOR YOUR HELP.**
Please check that you have included all relevant information and
**return the questionnaire AS SOON AS POSSIBLE.**

---

# Appendix D: The Graduate Questionnaire

N.B. This questionnaire was originally A4 and has been photo reduced for reproduction in this volume.

# CATE COUNCIL FOR THE ACCREDITATION OF TEACHER EDUCATION

# Graduate Questionnaire
# on Initial Teacher Training
# for the Teaching of Reading

## Aims and Objectives

The aim of this survey is to gather information about how students are prepared to teach reading in primary and secondary schools. It is being undertaken by the National Foundation for Educational Research on behalf of the Council for the Accreditation of Teacher Education (CATE) which has been asked by the Secretary of State to report on training for the teaching of reading.

We realise that completion of this questionnaire will take up time and attention at what may well be a busy time for you. It is desirable, however, that the fullest possible information about how teachers are prepared to teach reading is available to CATE, and your help in providing that information will be very much appreciated.

## Code of Practice

The answers you provide to the questionnaire will be treated in strict confidence. No individual, course or institution will be identified in NFER's report to CATE, or in any report or publication arising from the research.

## Returning the Questionnaire

Please complete the questionnaire and return it to us in its reply paid envelope BY 30 SEPTEMBER 1991:

CATE Enquiry
National Foundation for Educational Research
The Mere
Upton Park
Slough SL1 2DQ

If you have any queries, please contact either Greg Brooks or Alison Tate at NFER, Tel: (0753) 574123.

## THANK YOU FOR YOUR HELP.

2015 National Foundation for Educational Research in England and Wales

## About you

Please circle the relevant number or write in the information that applies to you.

1.  **Are you now in a teaching post in the U.K.?**  YES  1

    NO  2

    6

2.  **If your answer to question 1 was YES, please give the following information. If it was NO go on to Q3.**

    7 - 8

    (a)  age-range of pupils you teach:  ☐ yrs to  ☐ yrs

    9 - 10

    (b)  are you responsible for teaching reading to any of the age-groups mentioned in your answer to question 2(a)?

    YES  1

    NO  2

    11

We would like to know your opinions about the course you completed in **Summer 1991**

3.  **At the end of your course, how confident did you feel about the following areas?**

    (For each item please circle one number)

| | Very confident | Fairly confident | Not very confident | Not at all confident | |
|---|---|---|---|---|---|
| (a)  knowledge about language | 1 | 2 | 3 | 4 | 12 |
| (b)  knowledge about the process of reading | 1 | 2 | 3 | 4 | 13 |
| (c)  knowledge about methods of teaching reading | 1 | 2 | 3 | 4 | 14 |
| (d)  practice in the application of this knowledge in the classroom | 1 | 2 | 3 | 4 | 15 |

4.  **What approaches to reading were you taught about in your recent course?**

    16 - 17

    ...................................................................................................................

    18 - 19

    ...................................................................................................................

    20 - 21

    ...................................................................................................................

    22 - 23

    24 - 25

1

**5.** What were you taught in your course about phonic approaches to reading?

26 - 27

..................................................................................................................

28 - 29

..................................................................................................................

30 - 31

..................................................................................................................

32 - 33

34 - 35

**6.** In your opinion, was your course work (lectures, seminars, essays, private study, etc.) well integrated with your school experience in relation to the following areas?

**(For each item please circle one number)**

| | Very well | Fairly well | Slightly | Not at all | |
|---|---|---|---|---|---|
| (a) methods of teaching reading | 1 | 2 | 3 | 4 | 36 |
| (b) materials used | 1 | 2 | 3 | 4 | 37 |
| (c) the assessment of reading | 1 | 2 | 3 | 4 | 38 |

**7.** Please look at the following list of aspects of reading covered in some teacher training courses and, for each, indicate:

(a) if it was covered in your course

(b) how confident you feel about teaching this aspect of reading

**(Please indicate YES or NO and for each item please circle one number)**

| | | Covered in course/not covered in course | Very confident | Fairly confident | Not very confident | Not at all confident | |
|---|---|---|---|---|---|---|---|
| (i) | using children's literature | YES/NO | 1 | 2 | 3 | 4 | 39 |
| (ii) | links with writing and talking | YES/NO | 1 | 2 | 3 | 4 | 40 |
| (iii) | selecting, sequencing or combining approaches to the teaching of reading | YES/NO | 1 | 2 | 3 | 4 | 41 |
| (iv) | developing and extending pupil's reading | YES/NO | 1 | 2 | 3 | 4 | 42 |
| (v) | information and study skills | YES/NO | 1 | 2 | 3 | 4 | 43 |

2

| | | Covered in course/not covered in course | Very confident | Fairly confident | Not very confident | Not at all confident | |
|---|---|---|---|---|---|---|---|
| (vi) | identifying pupils with educational needs (including dyslexia) | YES/NO | 1 | 2 | 3 | 4 | 44 |
| (vii) | reading in specific subject areas | YES/NO | 1 | 2 | 3 | 4 | 45 |
| (viii) | assessing reading progress | YES/NO | 1 | 2 | 3 | 4 | 46 |
| (ix) | knowing where to obtain help | YES/NO | 1 | 2 | 3 | 4 | 47 |

8.  Are there any other aspects of teaching reading in regard to which you would have liked to have had more help during your course?

48 - 49

.............................................................................................................................

50 - 51

.............................................................................................................................

52 - 53

.............................................................................................................................

54 - 55

56 - 57

9.  Please use this space for further comments on any issues in the questionnaire, if you wish.

.............................................................................................................................

58 - 59

.............................................................................................................................

60 - 61

.............................................................................................................................

62 - 63

.............................................................................................................................

64 - 65

.............................................................................................................................

66 - 67

THANK YOU VERY MUCH FOR YOUR HELP.
Please check that you have included all relevant information and return the questionnaire
AS SOON AS POSSIBLE.